'THE WORCESTER PATCH'

AND THE LAST STEAM-AGE SIGNALMEN

MATTHEW W. MORGAN

Noodle Books

N.B.

© Matthew Morgan and Noodle Books 2010

ISBN 978-ISBN 978-1-906419-21-9

First published in 2010 by Kevin Robertson
under the NOODLE BOOKS imprint
PO Box 279
Corhampton
SOUTHAMPTON
SO32 3ZX

www.kevinrobertsonbooks.co.uk

Printed in England by The Information Press

Front cover - *Worcester Tunnel Junction Up Main home signals. Left to right these are No. 22 (to Up Goods), No. 5 (Up Main home with Worcester Shrub Hill Station distant beneath), and No. 7 (to Down Droitwich Loop with Henwick distant beneath). No. 22 signal formerly had a mechanical stencil indicator (sometimes referred to as a cash register), as this led to one of two different avoiding lines. No. 5 is in the 'off' position for a Cardiff bound service. See diagram on page 70.*

Adrian Putley

Preceding page - *The branch homes at Shrub Hill Jct, allow entrance to the station limits on the up or down platform lines and also protects the actual junction with the OWW line. The former signal in this location once protected the flat crossing of the city's 'vinegar branch'. The 'calling on' aspect allows trains to move forward into an occupied platform. By day they are distinguished by the letters 'CO'. At night they display a white light and when cleared a small green light accompanied by an illuminated 'C'. This tells the driver to proceed cautiously as far as the line is clear. 'Shunt ahead' signals look similar but display the letter 'S'.*

CONTENTS

SETTING THE SCENE

Once upon a time all young lads wanted to be engine drivers. Now, I imagine, the trend is quite different. As a small child I loved the railway, and the speed and excitement associated with riding on the train. But when I grew up, I didn't want to be a train driver. I wanted to be a signalman.

At that time, the 1980s, things on the Worcester patch were as they were meant to be. The infrastructure had changed tremendously in the previous 20 years, but the role of the mechanical signalman had remained largely unchanged for a century. The reliable signalman was in charge, and safety co-existed in perfect harmony with common sense. Some locations were such unspoilt idyllic places to work that people stayed there for years and years. This situation was of course extremely fertile for the growth of wonderful eccentric characters, who made life on the railway very colourful. It was a good life.

I don't remember mighty steam engines, nor do I remember the altogether slower, kinder and better pace of life enjoyed by former generations. In fact by the time I did work for the railway, all the 'real' trains had gone, to be replaced by soulless, 'buses on rails'. But one thing remained - the mechanical signalboxes lingered on, and the way of life that went with them. The all Great Western Worcester patch, though only a shadow of its former self, was an oasis of tradition amidst a progressing world. Many more Victorian and Edwardian signalboxes exist than you may realise, but so often today they have been stripped of nearly all their equipment, and stuffed full of microwaves, water coolers and other domestic appliances. Fortunately all those left on this district are instantly recognisable as signalboxes, and still do the job for which they were originally intended, many over 100 years ago.

Modern managements have tirelessly striven to eradicate all traces of the 'old' regime. Experienced signalmen are being replaced with 'computer assessed signallers.' However elements of the 'old railway' lived on in my local area long after British Railways did. It was this railway I was proud to be part of. In a short time I met some truly interesting, loyal railwaymen, who taught me about real railway work, and enriched my learning with cautionary tales, and hilarious tall stories. I became even more interested in this 'old' railway and its signalling. What I could no longer experience for myself I more than made up for, by reading about, or asking those old enough to remember. These 'old' things are what keep the trains running at Worcester, and have outlived the clever hi-tech replacements which claimed to make them obsolete. It is these 'old' things that this book documents.

The signalboxes of Worcester and the Cotswolds still stand and can be seen by all who pass by. They are living history, from an age when keeping the brass highly polished was almost as important as keeping the trains on time, and cabins doubled up as bicycle repair workshops or a barber's salon!

Alongside explaining a bit about the technicalities and the development of the 'boxes purpose and function, I have included my personal story and a few anecdotes in an attempt to illustrate what life was like as one of the last steam-age signalmen.

One day, when the funds are discovered, the whole lot will be wiped away and the trains will be controlled by a computer screen somewhere. I can't see that holding much interest for anyone. But as one retired railway employee told me sincerely, "they can take away this place, they could even close the whole line down, but they'll never take my wonderful memories". These are just some of mine.

The Worcester Patch

Today's Worcester patch is a large part of the old Oxford Worcester and Wolverhampton (OWW) and the Worcester and Hereford (W&H) railway companies. Merged into the West Midlands railway in 1860 and absorbed by the Great Western Railway (GWR) in 1863, it later came within the Bristol division of the Western region (WR), British Railways, and remains so under Network Rail.

The signalboxes on the area are a mixture of contractor built designs from before the turn of the last century, GW standard designs, and one WR prefabricated design. Few are the location's original signalbox; most have replaced a simple cabin from the earliest days of interlocking frames. The current lever frames are all ex-GW designs, although some are under 50 years old. Electric locks have been fitted to many levers, but essentially it is still mechanical interlocking between the

Opposite - *The Up Main home signals at Worcester Tunnel Junction looking towards Worcester, prior to the lines diverging for Shrub Hill and Foregate Street stations. The post is of WR tubular type, with 4-foot arms on the passenger carrying main lines and a 3-foot arm on the left: the latter referring to the goods line. Notice both the distant signals are fixed at caution. On the lower part of the post is the metal number plate indicating 'TJ', the prefix for the controlling signal box, Worcester Tunnel Junction, just visible through Rainbow Hill Tunnel.*

Adrian Putley

'THE WORCESTER PATCH'

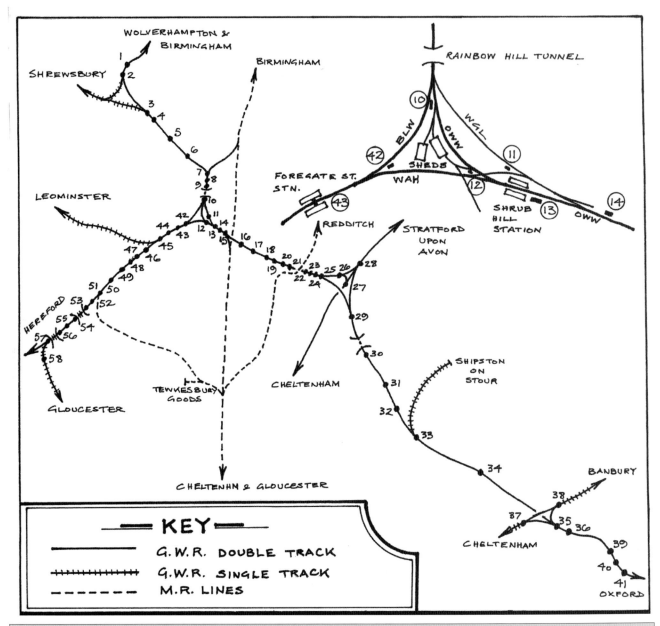

KEY
— G.W.R. DOUBLE TRACK
+++++++ G.W.R. SINGLE TRACK
-------- M.R. LINES

	'THE WORCESTER PATCH' circa 1930 and opposite, in its rationalised state circa 2000.				
1	Kidderminster Station	12	Worcester Shrub Hill Jct.	21	Evesham South
2	**Kidderminster Jct.**	13	**Worcester Shrub Hill Station**	22	Aldington Siding
3	Hartlebury Jct.		*(Worcester Joint Station)*	23	Littleton & Badsey
4	**Hartlebury Station**	14	Worcester Wylds Lane Jct.	24	Honeybourne Station North
5	Elmley Lovett Sidings	15	**Norton Jct.**	25	Honeybourne Station South
6	Cutnall Green	16	Stoulton	26	Honeybourne North Loop
7	**Droitwich Spa**	17	Pershore	27	Honeybourne West Loop
8	Fernhill Heath	18	Fladbury	28	Honeybourne East Loop
9	Blackpole Sidings	19	Charlton Siding	29	Honeybourne South Loop
10	**Worcester Tunnel Jct.**	20	Evesham North	30	Campden
11	Worcester Goods Yard	20A	**Evesham (WR)**	31	Blockley

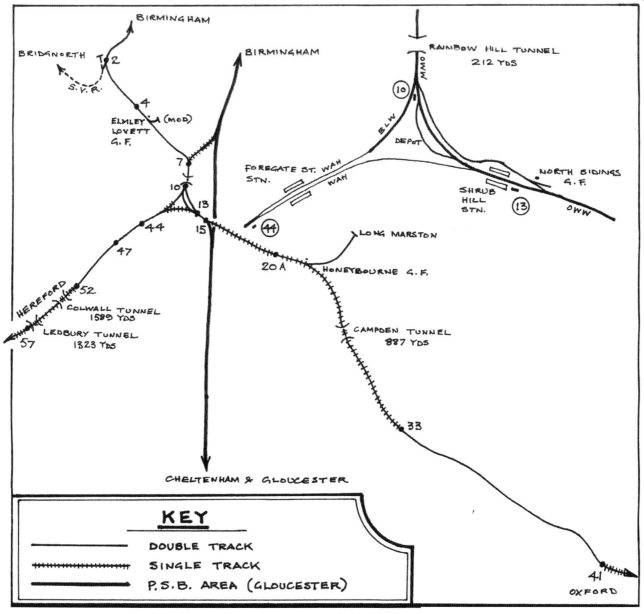

32	Aston Magna	43	Foregate Street Station	52	**Malvern Wells**
33	**Moreton-in-Marsh**	44	**Henwick**	53	Malvern Tunnel Jct.
34	Adlestrop	45	Bransford Road Jct.	54	Colwall
35 *	Kingham Station		*(Leominster Jct.)*	55	Cummins Crossing
	(Kingham North)	46	Bransford Road	56	Ledbury North End
36 *	Kingham South	47	**Newland East**		*(Ledbury Tunnel Jct.)*
37 *	Kingham West		*(Stocks Lane Crossing / Newland)*	57	**Ledbury**
38 *	Kingham East	48	Newland West	58	Ledbury Branch
39	Bruern Crossing		*(Malvern Link Gas Works Sdg)*	*	Kingham was initially called Chipping Norton Jct.
40	Shipton	49	Malvern Link		
41	**Ascott-under-Wychwood**	50	Great Malvern		*Where renaming has occurred the former name in shown in italics.*
42	Rainbow Hill Jct.	51	Malvern & Tewkesbury Jct.		

Learning, the old way, the signal school at Royal Oak in 1961. Prior to this, or possibly even in addition to, there was a signal school at Reading Signal Works, although elsewhere men would also learn, 'on the job'. Even at the time the view was taken, it might be questioned as to the need for such a facility, the number of mechanical boxes already starting to contract as MAS began to spread it tentacles westwards whilst elsewhere the various closure schemes of the period also began to take effect. To be fair, the wages BR were able to offer, meant experienced men were leaving at an increasing rate and this school was no doubt an attempt at recruiting and training new staff. Whether as in the old days, they were already railway employees or totally new, is not reported. In the background the equipment is worth careful study, an ancient looking train plus a variety of double line equipment from single-deck Spagnoletti block instrument to a 1947 design permissive block and of course all lower quadrant signals. (The lack of single line equipment is interesting.) It is tempting also to wonder what might have been contained within the large wicker baskets? The fashions displayed by the students are a wonderful refection of the changes in society taking place at that time. A generation later the present author attended a similar classroom at the privately owned Crewe 'training facility': complete with model locking frame and plastic cased block instruments, but still without any single-line training.

levers that prevents incorrect or conflicting routes being signalled.

The drawing on page 6 is set c.1925-35 to incorporate as many signalboxes as possible. At that time all but the very minor stations had a signalbox, with siding (s) and a crossover, although not all were continuously manned; some could be left unattended with the mainline signals cleared. Many private sidings or works had a 'box to control access to the main line. The multiple junctions at Worcester, Honeybourne and Kingham had a 'box at each divergence. The mainlines were all double track, except through the tunnels at Colwall and Ledbury. All were worked by the Absolute Block system, as most

British railways were before multi-aspect signalling (MAS) schemes became widespread.

The Absolute Block (AB) system works thus: The section of line between two signalboxes is the 'block section' and the signalboxes controlling entrance/exit to the section are the 'blockposts'. The principle is that only one train is in one block section at one time.

The double lines are unidirectional, one 'up' and one 'down', (up being towards Paddington on the GW) so there is no need for the additional protection against head-on collisions needed on single and bi-directional lines.

Each blockpost has an instrument repeated at its neighbouring blockpost, on which the state of the line is indicated. Messages for block signalling are sent via single stroke bell, to a prescribed set of codes. The signalman in 'advance' - that is where the train is *going to*, controls admission of trains into the section by giving permission to the signalman in 'rear' - that is where the train is *coming from.* The instrument has three separate positions: NORMAL (or 'line blocked') when no train is signalled; LINE CLEAR, when the rear has 'offered' a train, and the advance has given permission for it to approach, (known as having 'accepted a train'); and TRAIN ON LINE when the accepted train has actually entered the section. The latter is also used if the line is occupied or obstructed for any other reason.

Blockswitches, where fitted, allow the blockpost to be taken out of circuit – 'switched out' – which bypasses the instruments and allows the adjacent blockposts to signal to one another 'through' the switched out blockpost and so one long block section is effectively created. (See diagram on page 17).

Initially these block instruments were only indicatory, but various interlinking controls have been added over the years. Firstly, the action of 'pegging' (turning the instrument's commutator) LINE CLEAR now electrically unlocks the starting signal of the 'box in rear, thus permitting entry into the section. Secondly, a LINE CLEAR cannot be given unless the distant and home signals of the advance 'box are 'on' (at caution/danger). This prevents them being left 'off' (the proceed position) from a previous move and a second train following through into an occupied section. Thirdly, once a LINE CLEAR has been given, the train must travel through the section, and correctly occupy and clear the berth (first) track circuit, before the system resets, allowing another line clear to be given. In certain cases a train, having been accepted may then be cancelled. In this instance a manual time release can be 'wound out' for about two minutes, to reset the block instrument. Many signalbox desks contain a homemade device of shaped wire allowing speedier rotation of this safety device. This system is often referred to as 'Welwyn control' in reference to the terrible collision at Welwyn Garden city in 1935 where 13 people lost their lives. The signalman gave a second LINE CLEAR into an occupied section, having forgotten that the first train accepted had not yet arrived.

Western Region Absolute Block, featuring full Welwyn control is really very safe against most incidents, other than deliberate interference. In the Worcester area, other methods of signalling have now superseded some AB sections. These various methods will be explained along with the individual signalboxes that remain.

In order to work the Absolute Block method in the 1930s, and to operate points by mechanical lever, the signalboxes' area of control was only the immediate vicinity, with a good visibility of the equipment as well as the trains. The area a single 'box could control dramatically increased with the invention of the track circuit, and motorised points. As early as 1932,

Honeybourne North Loop 'box closed, with control being passed to Honeybourne Station South box, just 30 chains away. Despite the technology for remote operation being available, it was still preferred to have a 'local' signalbox, other than at very significant locations (such as Paddington, Bristol and Cardiff) right up until the 1960s. Although some minor 'boxes (at intermediate sidings etc.) were replaced with ground frames, the number of signalboxes during the 1930s remained quite consistent.

Through the mid Second World War years, some locations were provided with lengthy goods loops to increase line capacity. This was again made possible by utilising motor points at the furthest end. One completely new box 'Sheenhill Sidings' was opened north of Honeybourne, to facilitate connections to a depot there. It closed in 1951 after only 9 years service.

During the 1950s a few more minor signalboxes were abolished, replaced with ground frames, or permanently switched out as circumstances altered making the signalling redundant. In 1953 the 'box at Kidderminster Jct was demolished by a derailed freight train. It was replaced by a big W.R. design, but only to control the same area of the flattened 'box. A year later, the direct Cheltenham – Banbury flyover was taken out of use, reducing the number of signalboxes at Kingham to just one. During this period the idea of a 'central' box was favoured for new schemes. Where, previously, a layout had been worked by a signalbox at each end, one bigger 'box in the middle could do the work of two. Malvern Tunnel 'box was abolished by simply motorising the points, enabling control from Malvern Wells.

In 1957, Evesham was given a new 'box replacing the original pair. In 1959, Foregate Street 'box closed (as the branch to the Severn wharf was out of use by '57) and control of the station area passed to the nearby Rainbow Hill box. Yet still the numbers were healthy until the rapid decline of the post-Beeching years.

By 1963 the regional boundaries had changed to make the areas more geographically based; initially they had been the old domains of the private companies replaced by BR. The WR gained the ex-Midland Railway (MR) from Gloucester towards Birmingham, but lost the OWW north of Droitwich Spa, at Cutnall Green. Under a road worshipping government, many stations were closed and all the branch lines were lifted, as was the sad story nationwide. Local freight traffic was lost to the lorries throughout the 1960s, and with no branch or local traffic, the Cotswolds and Malvern lines became mere secondary passenger routes. Nearly all the freight yards closed and Kingham, Moreton, Malvern, Bransford Road, and Ledbury junctions all became 'plain line'.

The northern section of the OWW was truncated at Round Oak Steel Terminal, four miles north of Stourbridge Junction in 1993- now all trains must use the Stourbridge extension line to reach Birmingham and the north. The London Midland region (LMR) 'midlandised' all of the equipment around Kidderminster, and so there isn't really any GW flavour left there today. (I have included these locations in the preamble, for reference, although they are not featured in depth as they now belong to another operating area.)

By the end of the decade, the 20 or so signalboxes that remained were at the few surviving junctions, larger stations and level crossings. Anything else that had previously existed as a blockpost succumbed. Curiously, this could well have been the saving grace that saw the surviving signalboxes preserved.

And preservation it was. The neighbouring Gloucester patch had retained extensive GW and MR signalling for most of the declining 60s. It was a larger, more complex area to control than Worcester. Therefore in 1968, the whole lot was destroyed. Almost 50 signalboxes were replaced by an MAS scheme controlled by one panel signalbox at Tramway Jct, near Gloucester Central station.

In 1971, the Cotswolds line underwent a drastic rationalisation, only one 'loop' line to the Honeybourne line (Stratford – Cheltenham) remained, but as a siding accessed via a G.F. Then followed the simplification of the Worcester triangle in 1973 and the southern end of the Malvern line in 1984. Lines were singled and the remaining signalling was thinned out even further, leaving only what was absolutely necessary to control the layout locally. As the signalling was now comparatively minimal, the WR saved 11 GW signalboxes and the lower quadrant semaphores. Any 'new works' concentrated the areas of control onto the existing lever frames.

Towards the end of the 1980s an MAS scheme for 'Worcester Panel' (including the Malvern line) was drafted. Around the same time, mini signalling panels in the station buildings on the Cotswold line were suggested. Fortunately, neither of these ideas got past the planning stage. As the cost of resignalling rose and the wages of signalmen didn't, it was wisely decided to leave well alone. Mass automation plans slowed down nationally, and from then on new schemes seemed to be implemented on an 'ad hoc' basis, depending on what needed doing, and where.

The 1990s gave mechanical 'boxes everywhere a new lease of life. BR presumably slowed spending with the prospect of privatisation looming. When signalling was renewed, it was often the trend to close the offending signalbox down and install a small panel in the adjacent 'box. This occurred particularly across the WR, and once seriously threatened the future of Norton Junction. It is quite ironic that young brick buildings were bulldozed and older timber cabins took over their job! The new private company, 'Railtrack', did not seem keen on investing in infrastructure, except for the main trunk routes. The durable, easy to maintain equipment at traditional old Worcester obviously didn't create too many problems, and was permitted to carry on as usual. In fact, most of the signalboxes were renovated and even improved in some way. All had their paraffin lit signals converted to electric lamps. Areas suffering with 'wire degradation' were rewired. The mechanical kit was built to last, and has many years useful working life left in it. As long as they are deemed cheaper than installing the modern alternatives, the Worcester signalboxes are here to stay.

Naturally, one may think that the Worcester operating area is not nearly as complex as it once was, or not as impressive as others (such as Shrewsbury) but it certainly is quite unique today - the last bastion of pure Western signalling on the national rail network. Whilst 77 'Western origin' signalboxes still survive in use on the national network at the time of writing, some with their GW/WR signals, the mechanical signalling area is often 'patchy', or the equipment has been bastardised by the LMR.

Whilst modernisations (undertaken as recently as 2000) to the 'boxes themselves have been less than tasteful, the signalling itself maintains under the best practices of the WR and the GWR before them. In the city of Worcester, there is not one multi-aspect signal or plastic-cased instrument to be found. Yet hand-made block indicators and wooden armed signals are working reliably day and night.

My Beginnings:

I always wanted to be a signalman, at least for as long as I can remember. As a child I would stroll with my father most evenings around a circular route from our home in Evesham, Worcestershire. The walk took us up a road known locally as 'Black Bridges' a steepish climb up an embankment and onto the bridge that crossed the railway line. There had once been several spans; over the MR line to Ashchurch, then over several sidings, and finally crossing the GWR line from Worcester to Oxford. In my lifetime, only the latter survived and the other spans had been filled in, leaving only one actual bridge and a desolate patch of wasteland where the MR had once been – although a few clues remained to betray the previous existence of the railway line.

From this bridge we would wait and look down at the ugly, flat-roofed signalbox, which had brown timber walls with grey flaking plywood boards around the top,

Opposite page - *Nearly all the equipment for the signal boxes on the Worcester patch originated from the signal works at Reading, the exception being specialist pieces, hand generators, single line equipment and certain pieces bought-in from manufacturers such as Westinghouse, much of this during WW2. With the contraction of mechanical signalling, Reading disappeared from the scene over a generation ago and scenes such as those opposite, within the telegraph test shop and frame fitters shop were no more. The skills of the men seen were similarly lost. Worcester is now one of the very few places where there remain a dedicated team of locking fitters.*

Taken in 1935 as part of the GWR 'Safety Movement', which might well be said to be the forerunner of today's Health and Safety regime, although it might be doubted if left to its own devices the GWR would have adopted such a regime as exists in this field today. Four-foot wooden signal arms as seen here, were once plentiful around the Worcester area, although nowadays replaced with the pressed-steel variant. The distant signal, minus a black chevron and with the letter 'R' for 'Relief Line' is slightly unusual. Reading 1935.

and a sun canopy above the windows. The end had a large glass pane from floor to ceiling level and so you could see the signalman walking about inside by the light of a single bulb suspended above his desk, which was mounted on the front wall. I was intrigued. What was he doing? Nothing appeared to be happening outside, yet he was pacing the length of the 'box, returning to the little desk, and then, as the train rounded the corner he would emerge from the 'box, exchange something with the driver and hurry back inside to replace the signal behind the train with an audible 'clunk'. Even though I had no certainty what he was actually doing during those bursts of activity and long hours of apparent quiet, I was quite sure that I liked the idea of his job.

As I later found out, although there was a lot more to the job than most people innocently presumed, being a signalman more than lived up to my childhood expectations – especially those early days of mine at Evesham.

Moving on a few years, to when I was 14 years old, the school allowed us one week to go and sample life in the big bad world. 'Work experience' it was known as, and there was no question where I wanted to go. Having enquired (by calling over the track through the open signalbox window) who the local signalling inspector was, I was surprised to learn that he had an office in the former ladies waiting room, on the up platform of Evesham station. So I went to visit the great man himself, with an ever-increasing sense of trepidation and practised in my mind what I would say. I caught him scurrying across the footbridge and hastily delivered my rehearsed speech, and a letter. He proved quite reasonable though, and told me to report to him the following Friday, and then hurried off into a waiting car. Without any thought of whether or not I could actually present myself at the appointed time – a school day – I rushed home to tell my parents the good news, that I was going to work a real signalbox, even if it was just for one week!

Of course it ended up being much more than a week. As I made myself known to the various signalmen, and avoided the various inspectors, I was able to go up to the 'box whenever anyone friendly was on duty, although I was careful not to outstay my welcome. Traditionally the signalbox has welcomed interested 'trespassers' and I'm grateful to have had that opportunity to learn under close supervision, and benefit from other's experience. It definitely stood me in good stead later on.

It was during one of my many unofficial turns that I first took charge on my own. The man on duty had gone to the late-night shop for provisions, promising to "be back in 5 minutes". A good half an hour later the down HST (High Speed Train service from London Paddington to Hereford) was put 'on-line' (Train entering section - 2 bells) from Moreton-in-Marsh. Nervously I waited for his return, as the train drew ever nearer. It soon became clear that he wasn't coming back. I contemplated leaving. Then I thought about it some more; I had carried

out the procedure countless times before after all. So I lowered the barriers for the crossing at Badsey, offered the train on to Norton Junction and cleared all the signals, noting all the times on a scrap of paper. So along came the train, and out I went (trying to appear as tall as possible) and crossed under the protruding nose of the class 43 power car to deliver the token to the driver. "Cheers chief!" smiled the Bristol man at the controls. With a surge of audacity I strode back up the operating floor and waved nonchalantly in acknowledgement to the driver's 'toot'.

Although I was pleased with myself I didn't think the authorities would be pleased to learn that the Cathedrals Express was being signalled by a schoolboy, so I decided it wise to avoid that particular signalman thereafter.

However, my visits by no means decreased. Thanks to the continued patience and good will of a couple of signalmen I gradually learnt more and more about the ways of the 'box. One, a resident of Evesham was happy to let me pull a few levers under supervision. As a sociable type, he chatted to most of the railwaymen and women in the area, and introduced me to many – previously nameless – faces whom I would later work alongside.

The other was a reliefman, and seemed happy to tutor me in the regulations, and explain in detail everything I wanted to know. With quite a few years service, he always had a first or second hand tale to recount for each lesson being taught. It's one thing to just know the rules, but far more valuable to know where they came from, and how they are applied in varying circumstances. I am particularly indebted to these two gentlemen for starting me off in the world of signalling.

And what a good basis it was. When I did become a signalman, in my own right, I already felt 'at home' in the 'box, and knew what was going on at all the other 'boxes. How worrying to consider that today's new entrants are given the minimum theory training, perhaps a computer based assessment, and then thrown into major power signalling centres to deal with whatever hits them. Being an advocate of the 'old way' of training I was happy to continue the practice of admitting sensible visitors, who were eager to learn the 'box. It provided a refreshing change to the time-wasting visitors thrust upon us from upper management! It also provided me with a fitting legacy to leave the Worcester patch – two of my regular 'helpers' now have signalboxes of their own, and have made excellent signalmen, entering via the backdoor so to speak, as I and many before me did.

In the spring of 1998 I finished at school, just aged 16, and commenced what I thought would be a long wait before I could be employed by the railway at 18. The wait was prematurely ended a few months later. Providentially the careers service wrote to me with details of an apprenticeship with G.T. Railway Maintenance, as a trainee technician with the Signal and Telegraph (S&T)

The Cotswold S & T gang. Left to right: Robert Finch, Richard Amott and Trevor Partridge at Norton Junction on my last day working with them

department at Worcester. Having learnt all I could absorb about operating the signalbox, I would now learn how it all worked.

After passing the interview, aptitude tests and a medical, I was sent off to Bristol for induction, and eventually started in the autumn at Worcester Depot. Nothing would have prepared me for the complexity of the systems I would help maintain. I had thought I had a rough idea of how everything worked, but there is much more to signalling than just the levers visible in the 'box. Track circuits, mechanical interlocking, battery boxes, treadles, AWS (Automatic Warning System) magnets, innumerable relays and fuses, yards of rodding, wires and cranks, and miles of unseen cable are needed to adequately protect the trains.

I was soon assigned – quite appropriately – to the Cotswolds gang of Richard Amott and Trevor Partridge, led by lineman Robert Finch, who cared for the district between Charlbury (excl.) to Norton Junction (incl.) and, if necessary, attended to faults anywhere in the Worcester maintenance boundary. This stretched from Droitwich Spa down to Ledbury, and also included the northern reaches of Gloucester Panelbox, from Blackwell (at the top of the Lickey incline) to Ashchurch, so the equipment was diverse. They provided me with first class tuition in all aspects of signalling, general railway work and tea making. I also learnt many alternative road routes through the Cotswolds, and where to procure the best cakes or fish and chips throughout the county. Sometimes the work was almost recreational, like strolling up to the line at Ascott with a trolley loaded with batteries, on a beautiful clear afternoon. Other times it was bleak and unpleasant, such as the day we spent 10 hours in the driving wind and rain at Abbotswood Junction, attempting to clear up flood-damaged point motors.

The job had a profound effect on me, preparing me for life and teaching me valuable lessons about pride in a job and loyalty to a service. Who would know that

battery shelves, hidden in remote line side cupboards, are dusted and polished as highly as the mantelpiece of a front parlour? The gang had a strong sense of ownership of their district, and that was reflected in the reliability of the equipment they strove to keep well maintained. On the rare occasions a fault did occur, the gangs would often be called out from home to remedy the problem without delay

Occasionally I went out with other gangs (Mr. Finch's brother Geoff looked after the Malvern district) all of them were friendly and knowledgeable, but I was always happiest on the Cotswolds.

Although it was accepted that one day I would leave the S&T to pursue a career in the upstairs of the signalbox, it all happened quite by surprise, as had my initial entry to the railway service. Whilst waiting on the platform at Evesham one morning, for my train into work I met the Cotswolds signalling inspector Pat Crowther. It was the same man on the same footbridge I had come across 3 years before as a schoolboy.

He scurried across the bridge, in his usual

Local signalman Dave Pagett depicted here on duty in Shrub Hill Station box.

fashion, nodding in acknowledgement of me, but then made an abrupt halt. "I thought you wanted to be a signalman?" he asked accusingly. I said I did, but pointed out that I had not yet reached the required age. He regained his normal pace towards the platform gate, "Never mind, put your form in….you'll be old enough by the time they sort you out!" his last words disappearing with him around the corner.

It all seemed rather soon to me; but I quickly dismissed that thought with the prospect of my dream becoming a reality. The company (Railtrack at the time) had a curious way of welcoming potential employees by automatically sending them a 'thanks, but no thanks' letter. I had been assured though that the matter was in hand, and within 24 hours of receiving the letter, I received a telephone call from Swindon Personnel office with details of my initiation tests.

The interview was extraordinary. The Worcester inspector, one Mr. Lloyd, was to conduct the questions in his little hut at Worcester's Midland Yard. He never once rose from his office chair, but wheeled himself up and down the room, opening drawers, throwing paperballs within a 6 feet radius of the bin, and generally portraying an air of chaos. He hardly seemed to notice me enter at all, until eventually he turned to me, red-faced, spluttering "sit down, sit down, now…. Pat wants you, so you'll be alright as long as you don't cock it up with the H.R. (human resources dept)"

Just then a lady in a business suit and large silver Mercedes drew up, bringing with her a glimpse of the 'other half' of the company. I'm quite sure that the woman from the big office was so stunned by the abrasive manner of the inspector, and his little hut, that she forgot all about me, and my answers to her seemingly random questions. I just about made it through without laughing at the inspector's inappropriate comments towards her interviewing technique. At one point he guffawed "What kind of a stupid question is that?!.....All I'm interested in is can you get up in the morning?" I thought he was wonderful, but clearly she was not amused. The melodic clanking of shunting outside continued distractingly, and the room vibrated with the passage of each train, and the inspector's chair. All the while I could hear the levers in the adjacent Station 'box crashing back and forth, and the cacophony of block bells through the open window. But for once I paid no attention, and purely concentrated on getting through the ordeal.

And so I was sent off to Crewe for 8 weeks to learn the rules and regulations for train signalling by Absolute and Track Circuit Block. Then, at last, I went back home to Evesham – and the real learning started. And so we shall take a trip along the Worcester Patch, which commences at a remote outpost in Oxfordshire…..

The Norton Gnomes. These gnomes, which belonged to Alan Gibson (Norton signalman until 2002) were christened Bob, Dick, Trev and Matty after the S&T gang - photographed on the opposite page. There was also a plastic dinosaur that occasionally leaned over from the top of the plant pot. We called him after the S&T supervisor! They were still present the last time I passed Norton on the train.

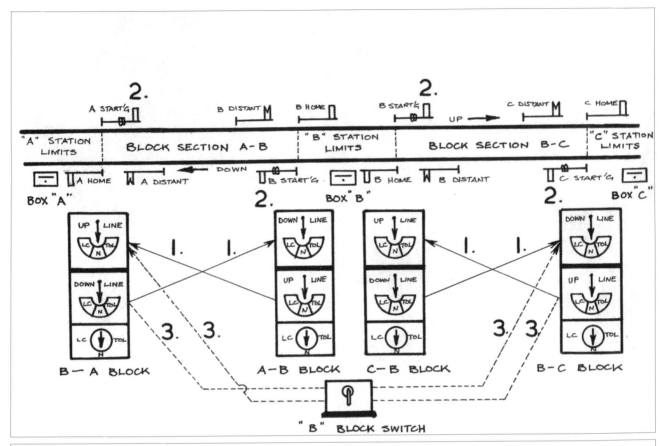

The diagram shows a section of line signalled under the 'Absolute Block' regulations, controlled by three signal boxes ('A', 'B' and 'C'.) The 'block section' is the line between the starting signal of the box in rear, to the home signal of the box in advance. (i.e. the direction in which the train will travel). The instruments show the state of the section, viz, NORMAL (no train signalled - arrow on instrument pointing down). LINE CLEAR (when a train has been accepted). 'TRAIN ON LINE (when the train is in the actual section).

1.   The indication is repeated from the controlling signalman to the signalman in rear.
2.   This electrically releases the starting signal into the forward section.
3.   When box 'B' switches out of circuit (having cleared all his relevant signals), box 'A' communicates directly with box 'C' forming a single block section between 'A' and 'C'.

A more detailed explanation is found on pages 8 and 9.

Ascott-Under-Wychwood signalbox, facing Oxford. The exterior of the box is well kept and has been thoughtfully repainted. The charming village is behind the trees, to the right, and the toad pond (see text) is to the left. The station was once adorned by flowers, tended by a now retired signalman. Up until 1989 it regularly won the best kept station in its area for the 'unmanned' category - although of course the signalman was always there to look after the place. The short platform means that normally only 2 car trains may call there, by request.

2

Ascott-Under-Wychwood

S ituated 80 miles 36 chains from Paddington is Ascott-under-Wychwood, the first traditional 'box on the OWW route, 'fringing' with Oxford panel signalbox. Built in 1883, it is classified a GW4b, a design which could once be found at several locations along the line. Today just one other example remains in the Cotswolds. The 'box does not house the original frame, but a 25 lever GW 5VT from c.1949. Seven levers are in use, several remain as spare.

When the signalling was rationalised in the late '60s/early '70s this 'box was retained, presumably as it controlled a level crossing and so some form of signalling would have had to remain there. The neighbouring Shipton and Charlbury were blockposts with station sidings and were dispensed with in 1965 and 1971 respectively.

Bruern Crossing Ground Frame, just less than three miles away towards Worcester was a gatebox (as of 31st October 1971) and as such did not control trains directly or shorten the block section. So in 1973, control was passed to Ascott via CCTV surveillance and remote controlled barriers.

Today, the building may be considered ancient (and does lean somewhat) but the signalling is comparatively modern, all but one signal being colour light, and full track circuiting provided in the station limits. The distant signals work automatically from the corresponding home signal. The electrical interlocking (via relays) directly controls the colour light signal aspects, rather than the more traditional method of electro-mechanically locking the controlling lever. The initial relocking for the route's singling utilised semaphores; much of the original frame and the gates were wheel worked, but all that changed when lifting barriers were fitted later. Ascott-under-Wychwood was once under the Reading area (the old London Division), which may account for the newer standard of redesign, as mechanical 'boxes were scarce on that district (today they have just one at Greenford East). Ascott works Absolute Block through to Moreton-in-Marsh, and under track circuit block regulations from Oxford PSB. Treadle annunciators are provided at Charlbury and near Kingham, so the signalman can lower the barriers and clear the signals in good time for approaching trains.

The line from Wolvercote junction, which was singled on 6th November 1971, is under the complete control of the Oxford panelman. Ascott must 'ask' for a 'slot' (an electrical release) to signal an up train to him. Trains in the down direction enter the section at Wolvercote with no action or authority from the Ascott man under normal operating conditions – though a train description is sent via the block bell. Axle counters protect the single line section. A device at each end of the section counts the axles as a train passes over, which deems the section occupied and prevents any other signal to enter the section being cleared. Its 'partner' device at the other end counts the axles exiting the section, only if the two equalize (proving that nothing has been left behind) will the system reset and permit another train to be signalled in. A very efficient system, when it works. Occasionally it doesn't and working by Pilotman must be brought in. This is when one person authorises each train over the single line in person, and therefore can only be at one end of the section at a time.

Other responsibilities include the farm crossings at Lyneham and Hyatts which have a telephone link to the signalman. Also, it is now the 'local' 'box for Kingham and Charlbury stations and as such provides information to the booking clerks there when necessary.

During normal circumstances, the Ascott signalman has no real regulating responsibility, but simply deals with what Oxford sends. This may mean an up train incurring a long wait, but there is nothing he can do without Oxford's release. All this makes for very stress-free, enjoyable working, if not too repetitive or unchallenging. Most trains pass the 'box at speed, except for one stopper each way on weekdays (up in the morning, down in the evening) and a few more on Saturdays. There was a siding in the yard up until the 80s, but there is no longer any freight traffic.

So the Ascott signalman can enjoy quite a quiet life – plenty of time for cooked breakfasts, reading books and washing the car….

However any 'box can have its moments, and this place seemed to have more than its fair share in the period I knew it. During my spell on the S&T I encountered several failures which mysteriously 'went home with the signalman', 'run throughs' (where a train passes over trailing points which are not set for the move, and distorts/damages the point/lock fittings), rumours of a train being sent down the up line in error and a 'deadly embrace', where two trains ended up facing each other on the single line. Fortunately none of these incidents led to any disaster and were sorted out in a gentlemanly manner, but all led to the suspicion that the serenity of a quiet shift at Ascott somehow bewitched the signalmen into a false sense of security, thus losing their senses when something actually went wrong.

I went to learn Ascott in the spring of 2001. Due to its remoteness it was unpopular with some reliefmen, as most were Worcester based, and so had a lengthy drive up

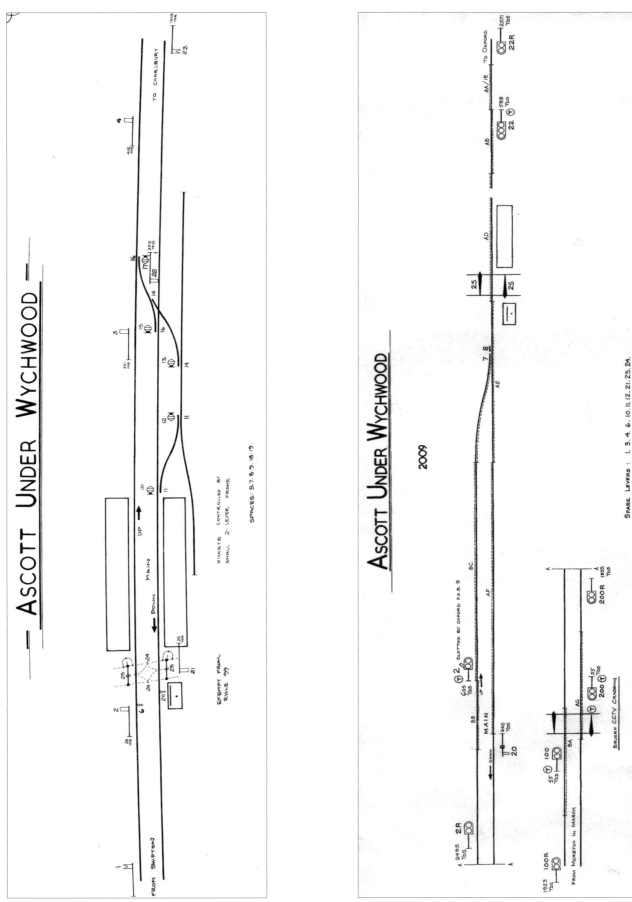

there on slow - sometimes foggy – lanes.

Therefore, quite a few resident men from the 'Cotswold end' volunteered to learn the 'box. It only took a day's training to learn the place, as I was already familiar with the local area from my S&T days, but I went twice just to be sure.

The morning man was Cliff Packham, who cycled to work every single day, and wore thick woollen socks over his trousers in all weathers. He sat and read quietly with classical music playing on his (banned) radio, seemingly bothered by nothing. His pipe was smoking splendidly, and often the smog was so dense I'm not sure he could even see his book.

The afternoon man was completely the opposite, interfering with anything and everything, and spent the entire time nosing at the neighbours and making 'enquiries' on the 'phone. The highlight came when he spotted some local lads messing about behind the station, but by no means on the railway. He produced an old fashioned, conical shaped loud-hailer (stamped GWR) from the top shelf, and bellowed out of the window at them to "go away at once". I'm not sure who jumped the most, the naughty boys or the old lady passing with her Yorkshire terrier! None was more surprised than me, clearly uninitiated into this way of village life.

A week or so later, the Inspector, Mr. Lloyd came up with me and asked a few questions. The relief man on duty at the time said "He'll do", and I was passed for Ascott-under-Wychwood.

To have worked there permanently would've been quite mundane really, but on a one-off basis it was quite a treat. The peaceful, quiet day I looked forward to rarely happened in reality though. It seemed there was always something going on whenever I went there that I hadn't planned for. Invariably my large cooked meal (which I *always* planned for) got interrupted, or worse, missed altogether.

On my very first day at Ascott, a morning shift, I was welcomed by a note explaining that a tractor had taken one of the barriers with it at Bruern crossing. A less than straightforward day followed liaising with the crossing attendant, the S&T, the on-call inspector and each train driver who had to be stopped specially and advised via the signal post telephone.

Nevertheless, Ascott was a charming place to work. I always loved the early turn, arriving in the dark through the mist, invariably far too early for the 5.15am start, fetching the giant GW key from its hook under the steps and opening up the 'box, which had been left nice and warm. I used to open the platform gate as well, and then switch on the station lights. I'd often pause in thought at this; whilst not as romantic as hanging out Tilley lamps it did seem to have quite a link to the old days of the porter-signalman. I liked the idea of 'my' station next to 'my' 'box.

The 'box was cosy, but not so small as to be claustrophobic. As the sun awoke, it would beam through

The equipment at Ascott-under-Wychwood. The CCTV for Bruern Crossing is at the far end of the shelf. The instrument for AB signalling to Moreton-in-Marsh and its bell (hidden behind) are in the centre. The dome shaped bell to Oxford PSB is used for train descriptions and emergency alarms. The pedestal, which holds the barrier controls is out of sight, to the right. The dominant lever colour is white; they are all spare, in reality redundant. The brown lever (in reversed position) is the barrier interlock lever. Previously it would have mechanically locked the swinging gates. With the introduction of lifting barriers it is now electrically released by electrical contacts on the barriers, proving them to be lowered. On being normalised (pushed in the frame) it mechanically unlocks the signals protecting the crossing.

the windows, reflecting off the shiny lever tops and brass bells. A special time to be in any 'box, but too busy at most locations to enjoy it, not at Ascott though. The rear window looks out over the honey-coloured village, which is very traditional with its small school and, of course, a pub. It was a superb vantage point to observe the comings and goings of the local folk, which were usually at a steady, if not sleepy pace. The front of the 'box overlooks fields, by winter full of sheep, by summer full of caravans and campers. Indeed, most of my time here was spent watching nature of one sort or another. My only upset was that the open fireplace had long been bricked up. To have had a glowing coal fire beside the chair would have completed the ambience to perfection.

The village was not unfriendly, and people would always wish you "good morning" as they passed, a couple of regulars even calling in for a cup of tea. The campers were even more sociable, the crossing being somewhat of a novelty perhaps? I was asked more than once for a photograph, or a turn pulling a lever. I did hear of campsite barbeques providing the signalman's dinner now and again, but I was not fortunate enough to receive such a kind invitation.

One peculiarity, which I have never heard of anywhere else, occurs during the amphibious mating season. Opposite the 'box is a pond which many toads return to, to spawn. At the right time of the year the road and railway can literally be covered in toads, reminiscent of one of the seven plagues of Egypt during the Exodus! Not only are there special road warning signs, but also a lollipop sign – TOADS CROSSING – kept in the cupboard under the stairs.

I do have some splendid memories of working there, in an atmosphere of relaxed, happy days gone by. Perhaps the most dramatic was when 5029 'Nunney Castle' came through, on a rail tour. Having mainly observed steam on preserved lines before, it was most different at Ascott where the linespeed is 100mph, reducing to 75mph at the commencement of the double track (though steam is limited to 75mph). On this day the driver was giving it all she'd got, and as I stood at the top of the steps I was ever so slightly nervous as the engine swayed from side to side, passing just inches away from me. A marvellous experience - one that would have been commonplace before the summer of '64.

The oddest thing I ever encountered was late into one night shift. I was nodding off in the armchair as all traffic had finished for the day, but was suddenly startled by shouting. I leaped up to the window and again the shout came, "groovy baby!" There, in full costume, was a man on the track dressed as the spoof film character 'Austin Powers'. When he saw me peering through the glass he made off up the lane. Shortly after, the rest of the party, also in fancy dress, left their venue and also journeyed across the line and up the lane. At least that reassured me that I wasn't going mad.

One's eyes can play tricks in the dead of night, amidst darkness and sleepiness. Yet despite stories of a signalman's ghost and alien sightings associated with working this 'box at night, the worst I ever came across was a drunk, wearing a wig and comedy specs!

Bruern Crossing Box. This former signalbox (1934) and then crossing ground frame (1971) once housed a 6 lever frame and gatewheel. The wicket gates and detonators were controlled by two small 2 lever frames. It now resides appropriately in the garden of the crossing cottage perpendicular to the railway. The nameplate is of the WR pressed aluminum design. It was applied when the 'box was downgraded during the rationalisation. Originally a GW cast nameplate – BRUERN CROSSING SIGNALBOX – would have been fitted. I wonder what happened to it?

3

Moreton-in-Marsh

Moreton-in-Marsh is the central 'box on the Cotswolds, located 91 miles 57 chains from Paddington. It is contemporaneous with Ascott-Under-Wychwood, being built in 1883, and is the other remaining GW type 4b on the route. It is not quite an identical twin to its neighbour, having only one central window in the rear wall (whereas Ascott has two to give a better view of approaching road traffic). In my opinion, the 'box always seemed rather small for its role. Simpler installations were provided with much more substantial buildings in years to come, but back in the 1880s this humble structure, packed -by today's comparison- full of levers was deemed quite sufficient to control quite a respectable layout.

Moreton is quite fortunate in that the creaky and worn 38 lever GW 3VT frame, dating from 1911, remains with a superb 24 levers still in situ. Until recently, it also housed a small 2 lever frame to work the detonator placers. The use of this splendid invention is being phased out for questionable "Health & Safety reasons", and so it was removed to accommodate telecoms equipment.

One of the modernisations inflicted upon all the Worcester area 'boxes, was the fitting of double glazed windows, which has destroyed the quaint beauty of this old 'box. It has also removed an oddity that existed for many years, according to photos' and a vague memory of mine. This design of 'box had the '6 small pane' type of windows originally fitted. However, just one sliding section at the station end had been replaced at sometime with the later design of GW window (3 small panes over 2 large). To my symmetrical way of thinking it always looked quite wrong - but still more charming than uniformity in uPVC.

Moreton-in-Marsh doesn't have the benefit of an exterior door added to the porch (as at Ascott) and so there's no gain in leaving the 'box door open to warm the WC before going in. Not pleasant on a winter night shift!

The reasons for retaining Moreton 'box, through rationalisation, are not instantly obvious, as in some cases. The similar style, neighbouring signalboxes at Blockley and Campden also controlled level crossings (an important consideration), had siding space and could have controlled the double to single line connections, shortening the now long section to Evesham. But these 'boxes were stripped of their status and became crossing keepers' positions (as at Bruern) in 1971.

Moreton remained an important station however, and to this day maintains a healthy number of regular passengers. For this reason it may have been deemed desirable to have the flexibility of turning and restarting services here, and to stable sets if necessary - although at other stations where this was the case, the 'box was closed and trains must now go elsewhere to change direction.

Once upon a time there was a proposed plan of truncating the line north of Moreton-in-Marsh, and so maybe the 'box would have worked the new terminus? All speculation of course. Even today the policy of closing 'boxes down is a bit of a 'lottery', for numerous reasons, principally the budget I expect.

The south end of the station remains remarkably unaltered, although the very long refuge siding was once a loop, installed in February 1942 as part of vast wartime improvements. All traces of the other down sidings have vanished. This area is exclusively semaphore signalled, and all the points are mechanically operated. The other end of the station is quite a contrast. Sidings into the loading dock (still standing) have gone, and what was the branch to Shipston, closed on 2nd May 1960, is merely a short siding behind the platform. The most drastic change is the main line, which becomes single immediately beyond the platforms. The home signal, to enter the station from the Worcester end, is now a colour light and is further from the 'box than the semaphore it replaced. The bay sidings at the north end were incorporated in this redesign, but removed at a later date, accounting for the 2 white 'spare' levers in the frame (all previous spares probably being removed in the relocking associated with the singling of the line to Evesham).

Moreton-in-Marsh really is the gem of the Cotswolds signalling, being so unspoilt in terms of the layout there. It was a shame then that the 'box was unsympathetically modernised, and was for sometime neglected. Most fortunately it now has a good bunch of signalmen who have taken steps to remedy this decline, by repainting for example. Perhaps the most noticeable improvement is the restoration of the GW cast nameplate, now resplendent in the correct colours.

Since 20th September 1971, working to Evesham has been by Electric Train Token (Block) or ETT, on the newly singled line. The system is cheaper and easier to install than full track circuiting, but is more suited to quieter branch lines than main through routes. In the 1970s the level of traffic was considerably lower than today, and so ETT was deemed sufficient. The system requires just 2 line wires, whereas 'tokenless' systems require more. Recabling the whole section would be a considerable investment, which wasn't undertaken, not surprisingly. Many believe the singling of track was a prelude to complete closure. Thankfully the line did survive (and has seen a real revival) but is now left with a system which is antiquated, yet extremely reliable and safe.

The ETT system works quite simply. At each end

of the section is a (terminal) token instrument, which holds a number of key tokens locked inside. When one token is withdrawn from the instrument (which requires an electrical release from the signalman at the other end) no more tokens can be removed from the system, until the token originally removed is replaced back in the instrument OR travels through the section, and is restored to the instrument at the other end. Therefore only one token can ever be 'out' at one time. Theoretically there could be just one key token (as the even simpler 'Train Staff' method works) but in fact there are several, to facilitate changing traffic requirements (e.g. five trains all in the same direction). Each token is engraved with the section to which it applies (MORETON-IN-MARSH – EVESHAM) and no driver (under normal working conditions) will enter the section without first being in possession of the token. In this way he can be assured that nothing will be coming the opposite way (at least not with the appropriate token).

A further refinement to the system, developed later, is that the lever for the starting signal is electrically locked until a token is removed, preventing the signalman inadvertently clearing a signal into a section for which he has not first released a token.

The plunger on the token instrument rings the single stroke bell at the adjacent 'box, as well as providing a release (provided no token is already withdrawn). So on being offered a train, the bell code is acknowledged in the usual way, and the plunger held down on the final beat, to enable the adjacent man to remove a token. The machine has a galvanometer needle which deflects, signifying that the token has been successfully removed from the opposite instrument.

In recent years, due to the use of multiple unit type trains, token exchanges with the driver must be done whilst the train is stationary, (without a carrying hoop) and so the Moreton signalman is kept fit walking along the platform to meet each driver who needs to receive or surrender a token.

In July 1978, the gateboxes at Campden and Blockley were abolished and CCTV was installed at Moreton-in-Marsh for remote operation of the crossings. The block shelf in the 'box now has a cluttered appearance, crammed with indicators of the more modern, illuminated type. Most are for the various crossing controls and the protecting (colour light) signals. The 'box is also responsible for 5 occupation crossings on the double section towards Ascott and one between Blockley and Campden, which are seasonally used by farmers.

The Shipston siding (officially the 'Up siding') is often used to stable on-track machines (tampers etc.) in the course of engineering work, being a convenient midway location. Although passenger stock may be refuged there, alongside the platform, it is not signalled as a bay platform for passenger moves. The Down Spur (opposite the 'box) is also available for this purpose, but sees little use nowadays. On rare occasions an empty set may be 'put inside' to allow a following train to pass. The timetable at present usually allows sufficient time for a terminating train to shunt over to the up platform (through crossover No.18 or via the single line) to await departure, without needing to use the sidings.

I have never witnessed anything in the Down Refuge (long) siding, although if the need arose due to failure or mishap, it could easily accommodate a 10 coach train or HST set. It is a worthwhile facility, 'just in case' – whether the authorities will see it that way for much longer is another matter.

All trains through Moreton are booked to call at the station. Even if they are not in passenger service they must stop for the token exchange. For this reason, and also the reduced speed limit over the facing points, the colour light distant signals are fixed at caution, and can only show a single yellow.

The signalman at Moreton-in-Marsh has joint responsibility for regulating trains over the single line with the Evesham man. The old school signalbox etiquette generally gives the decision to the senior man. As Moreton also has a TRUST computer, which shows running information on all trains scheduled to pass, the Evesham man would usually make a courtesy call here before any out of course running. I was more than happy to make my own regulating decisions, as generations of signalmen had done before me, based on a great number of variables, principally local and regional knowledge. The situation today is quite different – the train operating companies dictate how and when they wish their trains to be run.

Moreton-in-Marsh was the second 'box I learnt, for similar reasons that I later went to Ascott - a bit of overtime and much more importantly, some variety in my work. There was only one resident man in early 2001, so the inspector was quite happy to allow it. My first impressions were mildly disappointing. The place was filthy, covered in dead flies, and the lever tops were rusty orange. Quite different to how I'd remembered it, and a stark contrast to my gleaming 'home' box next door. As the shifts were being covered by whomever was free, I suppose no one had taken responsibility for the chores. I knew instantly I would relish the challenge of getting the place polished up, and looking cared for once again.

There was a lot to learn, or theory to put into practice for me at Moreton. It was my first official encounter with Absolute Block signalling over a double line. I had been trained on the method at Crewe (and not ETT) but apart from a quick dabble during the odd visit somewhere I had not actually done it. I was quite conversant with the token machine, and its rather cumbersome bell plunger, but I quickly grew to appreciate the advantages of the standard block bell. With its light (Morse Code style) 'tapper', traditionally rung with the second and third finger (as opposed to the palm of the hand on a token instrument) it was well suited to 'rattling out the bells'. That was something I was prone to doing, and later became infamous for. Definitely more enjoyable

Moreton-in-Marsh signalbox, facing Worcester. The connection to the old horse dock is to the left, the on-track machine is stabled on what was the branch to Shipston. The Down Main inner home, No.4 is cleared for a Paddington-Great Malvern service. The rods which move the point blades can be seen leaving the 'box and running towards the south. Great care was taken by the S&T to keep the rodding runs free of stones and weeds – this was one of my apprenticeship jobs, armed with a suitable stick! I was most proud when one of the signalling engineers came to inspect the maintenance and ordered her assistant to photograph this run as an example of excellent work.

than the slow tolls that some favoured. I understand it was always considered poor form to tap too fast, causing the bell at the other end to 'click' instead of 'ting' as no one liked a 'clicker'. However the senior reliefmen I knew never seemed to worry about it, or 'clearly marking the pauses between the beats' of a bell code – as instructed in the regulations. It never caused a problem as the service was so predictable.

The other noticeable difference for me was provision, or lack of, track circuits. As Moreton's south end had not been recently resignalled or redesigned, the track circuits provided are minimal. They are provided where trains would normally be held (e.g. down home and up starter signals) and so lock the signals in rear, but it is quite possible to have a train standing out of sight, and not indicated on the illuminated diagram. To observe a down train approaching meant standing at the top of the steps and peering under the bridge up the line.

This wasn't dangerous of course, but occasionally embarrassing when a train coasted (under clear signals) into the down platform, and I – having missed its approach

– was not at the appointed place to give the token. Incidentally in this case I always thought it better to gently stride confidently up to the cab, and allow the crew and passengers to presume that I had been detained by important railway work. Running, red-faced along the platform would only confirm their misguided notions that signalman do nothing but laze about all day, reading newspapers and eating!

With a bit of experience at the ' box I soon learnt to judge the section time accurately (about 12 minutes with a stop at Kingham) and be ascending the platform ramp as the train poked its nose under the bridge. Legend has it that an old signalman at Moreton, now long retired, used to pull all the signals off in the down direction, lower both level crossings and leave the onward token on the platform bench for the driver to collect himself, so that he could nip over to the shop. It was only frequent complaints from Evesham that 'Train entering section' (2 bells) wasn't being received that stopped the business. One was never 'caught short' by trains approaching in the up direction. As a result of the alterations, full track circuiting

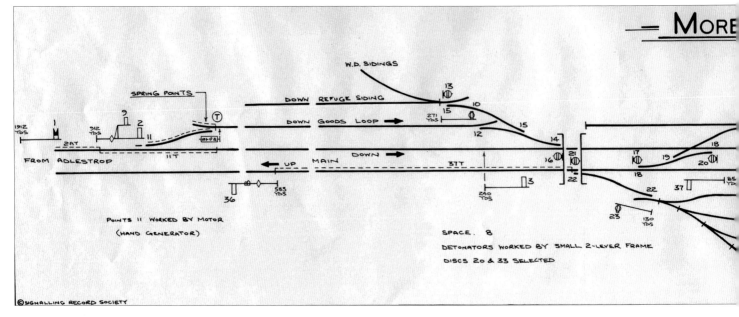

was provided at the Worcester end giving ample notice of a train. As well as aiding the signalman to observe the trains' approach, this also performs the essential function of locking the facing points, preventing their accidental – or malicious (!) – movement under a train.

The formidable Mr. Crowther came for my passing out exam after about a week's training on various shifts. I had carefully gone over all the Absolute Block regulations, and the special instructions concerning Campden tunnel. I was completely unprepared though for what he did actually ask. "Where is the key to the detonator box kept?" I took a guess, and said it was in the desk under the train register, aided by directive glares from John the signalman who was sitting behind. The inspector obviously sensed my hesitance as he peered up from his papers and stared right at me. "Show it to me" he said. There followed a panicking rummage through the desk's content in search for the key. "Surely he won't fail me for this" I thought to myself, (he always seemed quite fair, although very firm). After about half a minute (which seemed a lot longer) he broke his stare and waved me back to table. "Alright, alright, it's in there somewhere, now do these questions for me" he said, whilst thumping down his briefcase and removing a test paper.

It really was the most comprehensive passing out exam that this particular inspector ever gave me, but fortunately all was well. I was booked for my first early turn shift on 28th February 2001. Getting off to a bad start, with my Morris Minor 1000 arguing all the way up Broadway hill, I arrived close to time. It was a little daunting at first. Although it was not my first 'box, I still double and triple checked everything in those first few hours. As I began to settle in with a little more confidence, I knew I was going to like it there. I was right.

For most of the following spring and summer I regularly relieved there once or twice a week. It soon became a second home.

I always found the day to day work at Moreton interesting. When two trains were scheduled to arrive at Moreton together, it was preferable to have the up get there first. That could depart onto the double section whenever station duties were complete. Meanwhile you could go back to 'box, restore the token to the instrument, ask permission for the down train and (if it were accepted) clear the down line signals (Nos 2, 3, 4, and 5). Then you could be out on the platform ready to meet the down train.

If the down train was approaching first it was a slightly more laborious process. The down line starter No.5 would be at danger, since the single line ahead was occupied by an up train. Semaphore stop signals have only 2 aspects ('on' = danger and 'off' = proceed) so in this instance, or any where the train won't get a clear run, the signalman must ensure that the train is 'quite, or nearly at a stand' before clearing each previous stop signal. This effectively creates a third aspect: signal lowered on approach = next signal may be at danger (the equivalent to one yellow on a colour light signal). This technique, known as 'checking' a train, varies depending on circumstance. For example a heavy goods trains approaching on a downhill gradient would be given a heavy check, by bringing the train to a complete stand. Whereas a passenger train which is going to be brought right up to the platform starter may receive a lighter check, provided the train is making a controlled approach. This is when signalling becomes more of a fine art than an exact science.

This procedure has been in the regulations for many, many years, but now it has a more practical role than purely providing a visual indication to the driver. Since the installation of 'Train Protection & Warning System' (TPWS), maintaining a TPWS fitted signal at danger will automatically apply the brakes of a train which passes it. If a train did approach uncontrolled then better to have a run-by (and brake application) at the outer home,

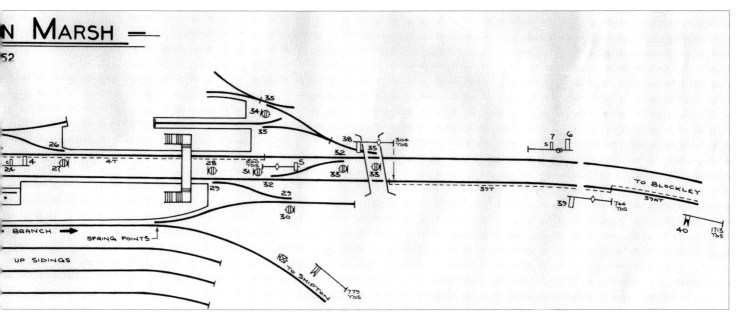

than to have pulled it off prematurely and have a collision further along at the starting signal. It is worth noting that on some regions this 'approach control' is designed into the interlocking (via the occupation of track circuits). The Western region did not opt for this feature, clearly trusting their signalman to abide by the rules.

When the down inner home (No.4) is cleared for the (now slowly advancing) down train, the mechanical interlocking prevents the clearance of the up home signal (No.38). Once this signal is replaced behind the down train, it is the signalman's responsibility to ensure it stops completely before clearing the up home, to permit the up train to enter the station. After dealing with the up train, the token for the waiting down train has to be walked to the driver. If it is a long train the rear end fouls the barrow crossing walkway and an extended journey along the up platform and over the footbridge becomes necessary. By the time you'd returned to the 'box the, now departed, down train would be rapidly approaching Blockley crossing and so no time could be wasted lowering the barriers and clearing the signals (MM100) otherwise the driver might be 'checked' with a yellow at the distant repeater (MM100R). I experimented with various ways of effecting this whole operation more efficiently, by trying to keep things always on the move. As most signalmen do, I found my best method of working, and then stuck to it.

Throughout this whole operation two sets of arrival/departure times and up to 5 bells signals must be recorded in the train register. Many prefer to accurately remember them (often all similar times) and write them in afterwards.

This whole business of safely controlling trains caused a seemingly enormous problem for the delay attribution clerks. Some had little knowledge of mechanical signalling, and relied on the signalmen to advise the cause of any delay. One can understand that the business of 'checking' a train could delay a down trains

approach by a minute or two. The delay clerks didn't understand the procedure though, and needed to account for the two minutes late arrival somewhere. One would think the fact that the train departed right time, or was held for quarter of an hour for the late running up service would eliminate the need for any explanation. Thankfully, I soon learnt more about the TRUST computer into which the times were entered, including how to input a 'reason code'. We received no formal training on this machine whatsoever, and had to rely on tips passed on by experience, as railway training always had done. Again one would presume that this reason code would reduce the amount of enquires necessary from delay attribution. Still, one poor chap telephoned me one morning, sounding exhausted, with the question "I see you've put Padd (down train) held due to the Hereford (up train)....How has a train on the up line delayed one on the down line?" I replied – in very few words – that there was only one line, and had only been so for 30 years. "Oh" he replied, sounding puzzled, "I'll refer that to the controller."

These conversations, and the inputting of train times for Moreton, Evesham, and Ascott did increase the work load substantially, yet the 'box was grade 2 (the lowest signalman's grade) as its neighbours on the Cotswolds. Today each 'box has its own TRUST computer.

In addition to trains passing through, each weekday morning an empty stock (bell code 2-2-1) would arrive on the down, from Oxford depot and shunt back into the up platform to form the first up service to London Paddington. On Saturdays, a passenger service would do the same, returning as an 'all stations Oxford' (bell code 3 -1). During these turnarounds, the driver would nearly always wander up for a cup of tea, or brief chat. It was then that I got to know most of the crews that I had only ever seen in passing before, although the station staff and taxi drivers must have been wary of me, a stranger. They didn't bother with me as they did the regular men.

Sometimes local passengers would tap on the door, mainly asking to use the barrow crossing (unofficially), or their children needed the loo, and couldn't wait for the train! I attempted to be helpful where possible, but sometimes passengers got too demanding during prolonged delays. On a couple of occasions, I was forced to shut the door, and the curtains, and hope that no-one ventured up the stairs. Sadly more than one Moreton signalman has been subjected to physical assault whilst innocently undertaking their duties. A shocking sign of the times, and particularly unexpected in such a charming Cotswold town. Nevertheless, I liked the people passing by or waiting on the station, as there was little else to view from the 'box – although I did once spot a monk-jack deer in the bushes behind.

In my early days at Moreton I spent a long time tidying up and trying to get those levers shining – no easy task. Removing the dead flies, which fell from the false ceiling every time the door slammed, was a never ending chore. I think they breed up there, and then return with a vengeance as soon as the weather warms up. Between trains all the rubbish which had accumulated round the back and the old papers could be burned in the big tin outside the relay hut. With the window open you could easily hear if you were wanted by bell or telephone.

One particular afternoon, to my horror, and embarrassment (in full gaze of the gathering passengers) the tin shot up about a foot in the air. There was an almighty boom and huge ball of fire, and then it fell, rolling over and discharging most of its semi-combusted content. Fortunately I had been standing well back when I flung the burning rag inside. I knew my father had warned me about the dangers of using petrol to start fires, now I knew why!

A few days later things got far more alarming. There was a driver who had been unkindly christened 'Sinex', because of his tendency to continuously discover problems, thereby 'getting up everyone's nose'. One day Sinex arrived at Evesham, and promptly reported that he had hit something in Campden tunnel, but could not be sure what but it "may well be a body". The tunnel was Moreton's responsibility, so the Evesham man correctly passed on the report to me. Having notified the booking clerk – to advise passengers – I put the kettle on, not much else one could do under the circumstances, but wait. A mobile operations inspector was summoned to inspect the tunnel on foot, gaining access from Campden crossing. The brave driver of the next up train volunteered to stop at the Honeybourne end and walk through from there. As the two men explored the dark, wet, unsociable confines of the tunnel, I went over the possible scenarios in my mind. What would they do if they found a body? What if part of the tunnel stonework had collapsed? What if they never 'phoned back at all? They must have got a small fright when they met each other in the middle. Neither had seen a thing so they resumed the examination as a pair.

Eventually they found the body, and contacted me to proclaim 'normal working resumed'. Fortunately it was not a human, but a pheasant who had taken his own life. The resulting delay was huge, and Sinex was teased mercilessly for weeks. To be fair the 'bang' when a train hits anything (including birds) is quite loud in the cab, he was right to be cautious I suppose. That didn't stop me smiling about it though whenever I saw Sinex.

Another drama to strike on a sunny afternoon was a bad case of tempting fate. A signalman friend, Paul Hale, had come up to the 'box to see whether he should apply to learn the place. "You've come on the wrong day to see any action" I told him, "it's all quiet here". He muttered a potentially dangerous phrase in reply, "anything could happen in the next half hour!" I must have agreed, and subconsciously confirmed it, by making the same remark to the next driver, who similarly noted that it was an unremarkable day. Immediately following that brief exchange of words I was gestured back to the 'box by my colleague – the 'phone was ringing. I attended to the departing train, following the priority order that an old hand had taught me, levers first, bells second, telephone last. It was the Swindon controller, "do you have any trains between you and Evesham?" I told him I did not. He then explained that the police and fire service were on the line at Aldington, as a car had left the road and landed on the track. It was not long after the road/rail collision at Great Heck (where 10 lives were lost) so I breathed a sigh of relief knowing that this would have a significantly better outcome. Simultaneously discussing arrangements with the controller I sent the 'Obstruction Danger' (6 bells – without calling attention) to Evesham and automatically 'collared' the down starting signals (No.5 and 30). A collar is a simple reminder device placed on the protecting signal lever to prevent it being pulled in forgetfulness.

As Aldington was in Evesham's half of the section I referred the controller to that 'box. Then I told Paul what had happened and boiled the kettle as there was nothing else to be done. Now, without passing judgement, it would seem that the mobile inspector who went to the scene had little faith in the brand new man at Evesham, who was known as "Zonk" by everyone except himself. The mobile inspector 'phoned on arrival at the site, greeting me with "right I'm dealing with you from now on, tell that bloke down the road to just shut up and do as he's told". I soon learnt an important lesson about being made into a 'go-between'.

When I was given permission to reopen the line I gave the clear instruction to my neighbour (from the inspector) that all subsequent trains must be cautioned, due to the remaining police presence. I included the need to 'drop a collar' on his starter. This last tip should have been quite superfluous, as every signalman – regardless of length of service – should instinctively know to use them, instead of relying on their memory. Despite all this Zonk decided he wasn't going to take advice from a younger man, and didn't bother, and then promptly forgot to

The interior of Moreton-in-Marsh. Having collected the single-line token from the London bound HST, signalman George Bryant now awaits the arrival of the next down train. The point and lock levers at the far end of the frame are in the 'reverse' position as the rear end of the HST occupies the track circuit: displayed by the illuminated light on the diagram. The Absolute Block instrument shows that the up train has been accepted by Ascott-under-Wychwood and that the down train is in the block section.

caution the driver of the next train. Having had a train pass the site at speed, the inspector called and was not happy, I don't blame him. As it was the days before recorded telephones, I gave Zonk a warning that I could not cover up any future memory lapse and all went smoothly thereafter. I felt responsible though, so from that day forth I adhered to the time honoured motto: "I work my box, you work yours." One cannot be responsible for everything and everyone, only oneself.

Remarkably the recovery gang did their job quickly, and the line was fully reopened, without restrictions in under 3 hours. That is when the work began; the trains had begun to queue back toward Oxford and now needed shifting. I had three waiting at Moreton alone, which made life more interesting. You couldn't really have that situation at any other location on the route.

Nothing very noteworthy happened after that, although Paul and I never uttered a word about it "being quiet" again! I treasured the remainder of my days at

Moreton-in-Marsh, especially those summer afternoons, often spent reading a book at the top of the steps, or just soaking up the sun, only interrupted by the bright ringing of the bells. After the ceremony of passing two trains the birds would start singing again, as the previous hive of activity returned to another lull.

Sadly for me, the 'box soon became fully staffed and I wasn't required much after that first summer of being almost semi-permanent. I was called back for the occasional night turn during the leaf-fall season, to run one Sandite train. I didn't enjoy that much. The 'box was cold and draughty when there was nothing to do, but sit still. I felt a bit like being in a goldfish bowl on nights. Being in full view of the station yard left me strangely uneasy for some reason. The illuminated repeaters lit up the block shelf at night like a Christmas tree, and the electrical equipment hummed irritatingly – not a good environment for snoozing.

All the signalboxes I worked were special in

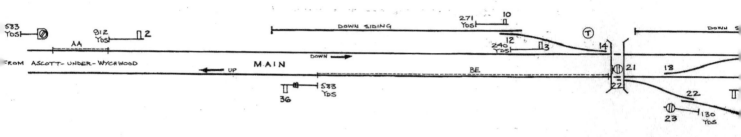

MORETO...

583 YDS | AA | 912 YDS | 2

FROM ASCOTT-UNDER-WYCHWOOD

UP ← MAIN

DOWN →

DOWN SIDING | 271 YDS | 10

240 YDS | 12 | 13

BE.

36 | 583 YDS

DOWN S...

(T) | 14

21 | 18

22

23 | 130 YDS

22

TEMPORARY SPARE LEVERS

SPACES: 1. 6. 7. 8. 9. 11. 13. 15...

MARSH

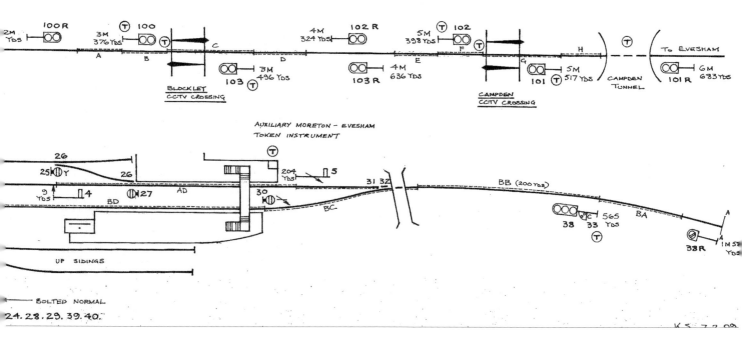

some way, but Moreton-in-Marsh was always my favourite; I think it was about as close as one could get to the old days at a small station. I often said I would like to go back there as a resident signalman before retiring, as those cold night shifts were rare, and those satisfying afternoon shifts were plentiful.

My final enduring memory of Moreton, which has nothing to do with trains, took place one cold and frosty morning. Having just visited the Gents and pulled the flush chain I stepped out onto the landing to take in the fresh winter air, and quickly became aware of an inauspicious rumble deep underground, followed by a pregnant pause. Wondering what would happen next, the silence was broken, and my question answered as the inspection lid blew off the sewer and the seemingly pressurized contents exploded upwards

and outwards. It soon froze hazardously across the platform. The resulting clear up operation found a shredded cereal packet to be the offending item in the drain. A wonderfully sarcastic memo from the inspector's office was soon distributed, asking that "only suitable items" were flushed down railway toilets. It concluded that anyone who was not sure what items were "suitable for flushing" must "seek advice from their colleagues." The sequel to this was an even more sarcastic, rogue memo (not from the inspector's office) stating that a competency standard had now been implemented, and designated "Flushable Items Officers" would be appointed and trained in due course. Although we have our suspicions, no one ever owned up to being the wag who owned the cornflakes!

Signalman Tom Mann 'pulls off' (clears signals) 2, 3, 4 and 5 for a down train. The provision of a false ceiling and replacement windows has drastically altered the appearance inside this ancient building. Note the erased parts of the diagram where the station sidings had been. The CCTV equipment dominates the shelf. The push button consoles control the barriers and camera equipment, the colour light signal switches and their indicators are mounted below. The left monitor is for Blockley Crossing and the right for Campden Crossing. The middle monitor is a spare and can show either location. In addition, each crossing has two cameras, should the first fail, and a local control unit should the barriers need to be controlled from the ground.

4

Evesham (W.R.)

The youngest signalbox on the district is at Evesham, 106m 76c from Paddington. In the March of 1957 it was the prototype of a new design for the WR, the prefabricated, flat-roofed type 37. Comprising panels 6 feet long, they could be easily dismantled and reassembled elsewhere, as many later were. The standard end sections incorporated a door for an external staircase, and so although this particular 'box had internal stairs there was an exterior door on both ends of the operating floor. In recent years these were blocked off, perhaps for fear that the signalman may walk out into midair! The principal difference - compared with all the GW 'boxes – is that the lever frame was fitted at the rear of the signalbox. This arrangement had been used by other regions for many years, but the WR did not adopt the practise until the '50s when the type 16/17 design came into being.

A brand new GW 5VT frame of 72 levers was installed, but the 1-30 section was removed in the early 1970s to make room below for the relays and equipment associated with Littleton & Badsey and Clayfield crossings. All the spare levers have been removed leaving a rather spacious, yet sparse appearance inside. The levers had been arranged with the mainline signals in the centre, and the (now redundant) points and shunting signals at the extremities – as latterly became the norm for large frames. It was this that made it simple to remove such a large portion of the frame, as no major relocking was required to 'shuffle' all the levers along. It was undoubtedly the smoothest frame I ever had the pleasure of working, which must be attributed to its age.

The purpose of the 1957 'box was to control new connections with the LMR's Ashchurch-Barnt Green line. Previously, the only physical link between the GW and MR was via exchange sidings. The new signalbox and junction made through running possible, it also made redundant the original GW North and South signalboxes, as the south (station) end could be worked by motor points from the now 'central' 'box. As the LMS 'box at the LMR station was still in use the new 'box was christened Evesham (W.R.). Although there has been only one signalbox in Evesham for over 40 years, the nameplate and 'box diagram (redrawn in 1971!) still bear this suffix. The new junction - which was not signalled to mainline standards, and had to be manually clipped for use by passenger trains – was used frequently by diverted trains during extensive engineering works between Cheltenham and Honeybourne. However it was a short-lived installation, as the whole Midland route from Ashchurch was closed in September 1963. I always liked to write the full 'box title in the train register, in memory of the days when my hometown was served by two railway companies, side by side.

The rationalisation scheme for the Cotswold route necessitated a passing loop on the long single line section. As previously seen with Moreton and Blockley, it was the 'box at the more significant location which was retained. Modern practice may have based the signalling at Littleton & Badsey's level crossing, not only did Badsey 'box have to be retained anyway – albeit as a crossing keeper's position – but it is closer to the midpoint of the single line in mileage terms, and more suitable for modern freight loading facilities. However, unlike the previous scenario, Evesham (W.R.) 'box and its lever frame was considerably younger than its neighbours, and so Evesham (complete with extensive siding space) was chosen as the passing loop location. The layout, as the diagrams drastically illustrate is quite different from the original. Only the up starter's large bracket (No.32) and

Opposite top - Evesham (W.R.) The line nearest the 'box is the Up Refuge siding which was once a running goods loop. The Tesco site behind was once covered by extensive sidings. This is probably the only mechanical signalbox that was aesthetically enhanced by fitting modern windows? The prefabricated, type 37 was built in many variations, for example some had additional side windows, some had external stairs, but all featured the up and downstairs doors and the sun canopy. The other working examples are at Bargoed and Whitland and are very similar to Evesham. There is a further surviving variation at Onibury. Built on a brick base it is only 2 sections long with half size end pieces. Surely the smallest, and I'm told, the hottest, WR signalbox.

Opposite bottom - The interior of Evesham (W.R.) The spotless, spacious operating floor is rather utilitarian. The position of the diagram and the empty block shelf, to the left, betray that half of the frame is missing. The short handled lever at the far end works the motorised south end points. The padlocked red box contains detonators for emergency use. Note the size of the diagram case which once contained an extensive layout. The three lamp repeaters are of the Spagnoletti design, where a flag swings behind an aperture to display 'LAMP IN' or 'LAMP OUT'. This particular trio is rarer than most, because they are not wooden, but cut from bakelite sheet. The most noticeable difference is that the glass window is circular and not square as per the more common type. In 1947 a new type of AB block indicator was introduced to replace the Spagnoletti type. These had the indications marked on the rear panel, and a needle swung to point to the relevant position. A matching type of lamp indicator was also introduced, both types can be seen side by side in the Shrub Hill photo: page 102.

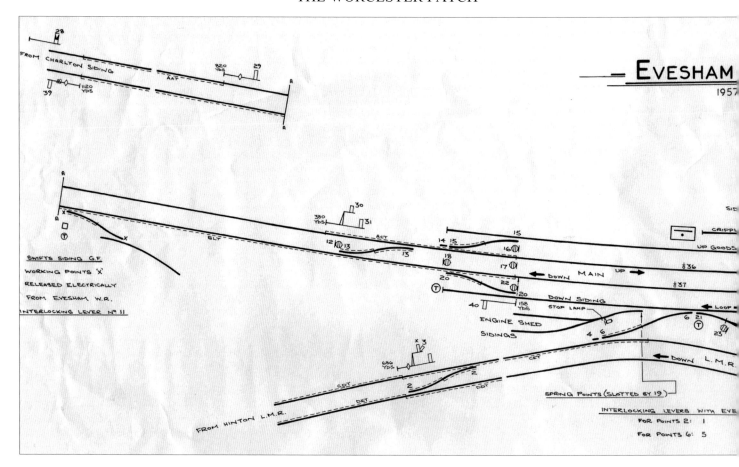

connections to the up yard – now just two sidings - bear some resemblance of what went before, for it is only a shadow of its former self. (Incidentally those little used points, No.54 were without doubt the heaviest I ever had to pull or push.) In contrast the station buildings have remained unscathed by progress, unlike many on the line.

The form is not exactly that of the traditional passing loop that could once be found on single track branch lines nationwide. The loop is much longer, the Oxford end points are motor worked, and the 'box is right out near the north end points. Whilst that was the correct location in relation to the 1957 alterations, it now seems – somewhat ironically – that the old Evesham south signalbox of 1883, on the end of the down platform would have been a much more convenient place from which to facilitate the token working.

As we have seen with all the crossing keeper's positions, CCTV operation made them redundant. Littleton & Badsey was closed in 1979 with control passing to Evesham. Clayfield Crossing, on a very quiet country lane was always worked by a resident crossing keeper, who came from the adjacent cottage and swung the gates as road traffic required. A continuous human presence was done away with in 1981 when an automatic half barrier (AHB) system was installed. Telephones are provided to the signalman, who can also monitor power and fault indications, but the operation of the crossing itself is completely automatic. There are no (railway) signals protecting such a crossing.

Additionally, Evesham has several user-worked crossings, on farms, footpaths etc. with telephone links to the 'box. One of these, at Charlton, serves a handful of cottages and is therefore used several times a day, others are rarely used. During harvesting season, several crossings become very busy, and so the telephone calls make up a large proportion of the summer workload. As it is impossible to know exactly where a train in the section is, extreme care must be taken when judging whether or not a user has sufficient time to cross. In the case of large, low, and slow loads, or animals needing to cross, the movement must be protected by signals at both ends of the section, though there are few moments in the daytime when the single line is unoccupied and no train has been offered.

After the singling of the Cotswolds route, the west loop at Honeybourne was retained, so that trains from the Worcester direction could access the tip sidings. At that time the Stratford – Cheltenham line was still in situ, and in use as a diversionary route for the Midland's Birmingham and Gloucester railway. When the GW line was finally closed on 1st November 1976 the Honeybourne West loop – Long Marston section was left to serve the MoD depot there. As all trains would now approach from the Worcester direction, a reversal was necessary at the

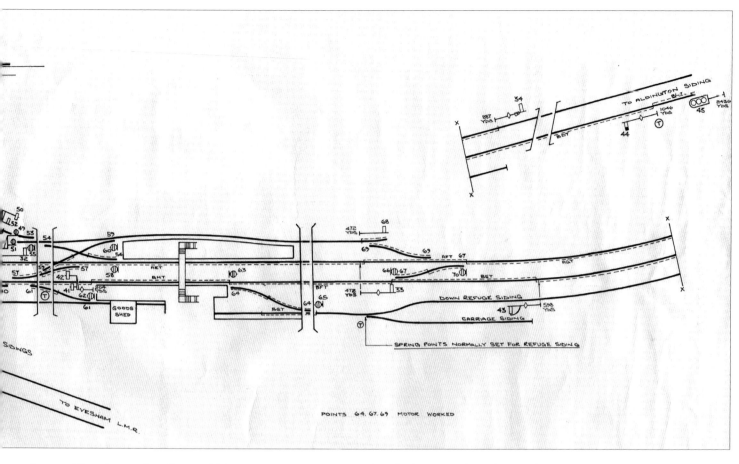

former West Loop signalbox, which was now a mere ground frame. In 1980, the sensible decision was taken to reinstate the East loop so that trains could travel straight into the depot via the branch line of almost three miles. The branch is worked by the one train staff method, the staff releases the ground frame at the Long Marston end, to leave the branch and enter the depot complex - which is under MoD control.

The ground frame at Honeybourne Junction, with the main line, is a simple two lever affair, released by the Evesham – Moreton-in-Marsh token. An intermediate token instrument is provided so that once a train has left the mainline it may be 'shut in' for scheduled services to pass. Before 1983 the 'ground frame' had been, perhaps, one of the most substantial on the W.R., for it was the decommissioned Honeybourne Station South Signalbox, which worked the junction points and associated signals. A frame which once had 57 levers, now released by a single line token.

The run round sidings at Honeybourne are supervised by the Evesham signalman, and today, the only signalling is 'stop & telephone' boards either side of the junction. There are no track circuits or indications at Honeybourne, and the signalman relies totally on information provided by the train crew by telephone. Electrical interlocking was recommended after an incident in 1989 when a train was reported to be 'inside and clear'

when in fact a portion of the train remained on the main line. The work wasn't carried out and is unlikely to be done now as regular traffic has ceased. Today the branch has no consistent traffic, but up until 1996 regular ballast spoil trains ran to the tip sidings. Periodically the branch is used to deliver or remove redundant rolling stock which is in secure storage at Long Marston. Trains to the branch are signalled as a 'Train stopping in section' (2-2-3). Once the train is clear of the mainline and the token replaced, the cancelling signal (3-5) may be sent.

The day to day work at the 'box can be simple. To pass a single train the routine is straightforward; all the relevant signals are cleared, having had the train accepted by the 'box in advance. The points would be set prior to accepting from the rear, not just in the interests of good practice, but as stipulated in the regulations for a single line crossing place – the line must be clear and all points set and locked correctly up to the loop exit signal. The distant signals are fixed at caution as all trains must stop for the token exchange. When token carrying hoops were in use the speed restriction was 10 m.p.h. - today all trains must come to a complete stand. On surrender of the rearward token, the driver can be handed the onward token, and the surrendered one can be restored to the instrument.

The barriers must also be lowered, and the protecting signals cleared for Littleton & Badsey crossing.

Token instruments at Evesham (W.R.) These are a later pattern of instrument and have plastic, rather than brass plungers and chrome plated fittings. There is a slot for a transfer magazine on the lower right side, but these are blanked off. Unlike machines on other regions, there is no indicator of the system status, but the older instruments (which these replaced) had a hand worked reminder needle which I thought was very useful. The tokens are painted different colours depending on the key configuration of the system. Highley signalbox, on the preserved Severn Valley Railway is the only place I have seen red, yellow, blue AND green tokens in use in one location.

There is an audible approach annunciator, which is actually an incredibly loud yodel alarm as usually found outside at such crossings (despite being smothered by a lever cloth the noise would still wake the dead!). For up trains, it is actuated by BB track circuit, for down trains it is triggered by a treadle not far from the site of the former Honeybourne South Loop junction. For a non-stopping train the gates must be closed immediately, for trains stopping at Honeybourne station (or those originating from Long Marston) the appropriate time delay must be judged. It is this that causes long delays to motorists held at Badsey crossing, or drivers to receive a caution (yellow) aspect at the down distant (E100R) unnecessarily. The preferable former doesn't have to be explained to the controller, the latter does. I was always taught that it was the railway that paid us to signal trains, so the train always comes first!

When two trains are booked to pass at Evesham the working is much more interesting. Having accepted both trains as normal, and worked the crossing for the down train, the signalman will usually judge which train will arrive first. When the down train passes over Littleton & Badsey crossing it normally takes just under two minutes to appear on the track circuit diagram on the approach to the down home signal (no.43). This track circuit (BBT) is 440 yards long so a short delay must be left before pulling off, to ensure that the driver has been appropriately 'checked'. When the up train has been in the section for about 10 minutes one would expect to see its headlight rounding the curve towards the north river Avon bridge. There is very good sighting from the 'box in that direction, including a pleasant view over the riverside fields and orchards, leading up wooded slopes to Evesham's manor house and the BBC's Wood Norton House perched on the hillsides.

When either train 'comes on the board' – on the berth track circuit - the signalman will either hold the train outside or lower the home signal to permit the train into the loop, depending on the circumstances. It is not permissible to allow both trains to enter the loop simultaneously, and so the interlocking correctly prevents this.

Usually it is preferable to allow the down train into the platform at the earliest opportunity. As the station is too far from the 'box, and the driver is still in possession of the EVESHAM-MORETON token, this is where some additional equipment and special instructions become necessary. Firstly the guard of the down train must advise by telephone that his train is complete, with tail lamp. Secondly the driver must return the token to the system by means of an auxiliary instrument, located on the platform. (This instrument is similar in appearance to a terminal instrument, such as those found in the controlling signalbox, but has no bell/release plungers, and has two galvanometer needles). On replacing the token, and advising the signalbox by telephone, the signalman is now in a position to send the 'Train out of section' bellcode (2-1) and offer the up train forward. Whilst all this is taking place the loop points will have been reversed behind the down train and the up train can be brought steadily into the loop. The up train can now make a normal token exchange and proceed under clear signals to Moreton-in-Marsh after station duties are complete. When the up train passes the 'box (complete with tail lamp) the signals and points can be rearranged, and the token replaced to the instrument and removed once more, in a similar manner to that just described, for the down train, which on completion of its station duties will trundle towards the 'box to await its forward token. Invariably, whilst dealing with this down train, and exchanging a few friendly words with the driver, the up train would creep away, leaving little time to return to the operating floor and clear the signal for the crossing (E200), so sometimes it was profitable to lower the barriers etc. before temporarily leaving your post.

There was a special instruction introduced during 2001, stating that if a down train is stationary at the down starting signal (No.42) the token must be delivered to the driver before the signal is cleared. This was a 'knee-jerk' reaction to an incident where a driver moved off as the signal lowered, without waiting for the signalman to deliver the token. Whilst this might prevent a reoccurrence of that isolated incident it seems to me that it could create more problems. It is not the method of working used at

The locking room at Evesham (W.R.) is home to a Great Western 5-bar vertical tappet frame and a couple of rats. The boxes below the frame contain electro-mechanical locks, (highlighted) the release of which is dependent upon track circuits and block controls etc. Beneath the frame is a deep pit containing the cranks and pulleys which transfer the lever movement to the associated equipment on the ground, hence the need for the gang-plank allowing (somewhat precarious) access for maintenance.

any other signal leading into a token worked section, so why adopt the practice only at Evesham, and only in the down direction? Of course one can easily predict that after 30 years of doing so, a driver might easily be duped into moving off (against the signal) having correctly received his token.

That is exactly what happened one day to a driver of many years service who was due to retire within days. There was no way I could let such a thing mar a lifelong career, so I positively sprinted up the stairs of the 'box, as the engines accelerated, and whipped the lever off as the buffer beam passed the post. As no actual run-by occurred, nothing was said. Following that, I always said "wait for the signal please" to drivers standing at the 'box. Most presumed I was attempting to be smart, or was covering my forgetfulness in not pulling off. Obviously nobody saw fit to brief the drivers to the change in the local rules.

Sometimes up trains are booked to arrive at Evesham a few minutes before the down train that they will cross. In this instance, or if following another up service, the train must be admitted into the station without the onward token. Another auxiliary machine is provided on the up side for drivers to withdraw their own token when it becomes available. The token hut is ill situated for modern traffic (2-5 coach dmus) and is well beyond the platform ramp, behind the road bridge - where an engine and eight coaches may have pulled up in previous years. The uneven walk to the hut in the dark was understandably unpopular.

Once the token becomes available the driver and signalman contact one another via telephone. The signalman offers the train forward in the usual way, and when accepted holds down his plunger (as the advance signalman is also doing) which releases the auxiliary instrument. The telephone cord in Evesham signalbox was extremely long to enable you to reach the token instruments at the far end of the 'box whilst speaking on the 'phone. One signalman even told me it was possible to dangle the receiver out of the window so a conversation could continue whilst sitting on a deckchair outside!

However a more normal length cable was substituted after the special one was chewed through, presumably by a passing rodent, (or was it a hungry signalman?) and so nowadays the signalman must stretch to reach the instrument without pulling the whole telephone console onto the floor – as I myself did in haste on numerous occasions.

It was always advisable during this procedure to ascertain that the starting signal had become 'free' before letting the driver leave the telephone. If it had not, the whole token withdrawal would need to be repeated, so I always pulled off immediately the driver announced that the token was out.

The local drivers knew exactly what to do and the system worked smoothly. Those who were less familiar made the whole operation into an ordeal. Every token instrument has a different 'feel' to it. The up auxiliary instrument at Evesham was incredibly stiff and needed both hands to manipulate the token into rotating its two quarter turns. If it didn't come out on the first attempt many would turn it back in again to start at the beginning, this was translated on the galvanometer as two deflections, so the man at Moreton would let go of his plunger assuming all transactions had been successful. You can't ring the next 'box when you are already on the 'phone to the token hut, and the bells do not sound if a token is left half turned - that is neither in, nor out of the machine. And so a lack of experience with the system could, and did create unnecessary delay, which seemed to instil a peculiar, irrational fear of the auxiliary instrument among nervous signalmen and drivers alike. Some drivers always opted to stop at the signalbox, no matter how long the wait, to avoid the nuisance of using 'the hut'. One even compelled me to walk to the station with his token as he felt "unable" to fetch his own, but the vast majority were very good, and the ancient old token block slowed no one down for more than a minute or two.

I went to learn the 'box immediately on completing the rules and regulations at Crewe. I had undertaken four days learning when I noticed that I was

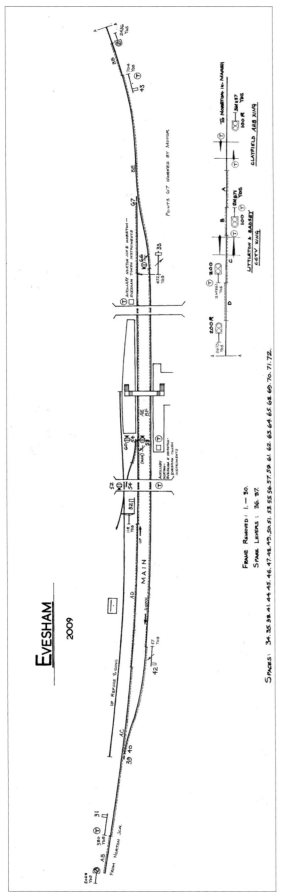

EVESHAM

2009

rostored to work my first shift the following Sunday morning. I had not taken any 'passing out' test to prove my competence, but I was told the boss would be along first thing to go through the formalities. I opened up Evesham (W.R.) signalbox at 9am on 19th November 2000 – alone, for the second time, though this time officially. The inspector didn't come until a couple of hours later. "I thought you were coming first thing to pass me out?" was my abrupt greeting. "Well you've done alright so far...haven't you?" came the even more abrupt, and slightly accusing reply. I conceded that all was well. After signing a couple of forms he was gone again, promising that "the signalman next door will sort you out if you have any problems". I realise now that the inspector was quite right to throw me in at the deep end, leaving me to do the job, thus building my confidence. After all, I had really been learning the 'box for the previous three years, I had simply arrived back at home. I don't remember much of the rest of that day, it passed by quite uneventfully. All I remember is being incredibly proud of my ugly plywood signalbox and wearing a fixed smile for every passing train, because I was now a signalman.

Life at Evesham was very sociable, and rarely lonely. There was always somebody passing through, and so the signalbox seemed to be a sort of congregating point. The S&T – my old gang – came twice weekly to exchange the tokens (which accumulated in the downside auxiliary machine and emptied from the upside), the Evesham permanent way gang called in on their way to or from a line patrol. The drivers might pause for a fill of hot water if the timetable allowed and the coalman came to fill his container from the outside tap. My Dad still took our circular route over the bridge of an evening and would wave cheerily whilst passing, and on a Sunday I was often treated to a roast dinner which was passed over the fence on a tray. All these 'regulars' made for friendly times, and due to the location of the 'box - remote from the station - we were generally free from troublesome characters as well.

The biggest bonus during my first year though was my neighbouring colleagues, there was a good bunch of chaps with Adam Sutton and John Harvey at Moreton and Alan Gibson and Craig Simmonds at Norton, and of course the drivers from Oxford, with the Worcester guards. Almost every day brought about another splendid jape of some sort, and I clearly remember walking home with a chuckle more often than not. I was told tales of tokens being covered in wet paint and then handed to the driver, only for it to then be heated up in the firebox and passed back to the signalman! Nothing quite as outrageous took place in my time, although I was once guilty of attaching a small saucepan to the token, in order to continue a long running gag with one poor driver nicknamed "Bubbles" who always ended up with culinary equipment being planted in his cab. I got my comeuppance though; the saucepan was not as well attached as it might have been, and he was able to separate the pair and hurl the pan at me before I reached the refuge of the 'box.

One day Adam Sutton heard rustling noises from the depths of Norton Junction's locking room. As was the custom he telephoned to discuss the 'occurrence'. One of the drivers had seen a snake basking in the sun at Norton earlier in the day, so between us (during token exchanges) we put forward the idea that there was probably a nest of adders, poised to slither up through the frame. Help was summoned and some brave soul from the contractor's company ventured in (with Welly boots and signalman's bread knife) to confront the venomous intruders. All that was found was a robin chirping away to itself. Naughtily, when the same driver returned and my neighbour at Norton sought confirmation of the snake sighting he denied all knowledge, adding that signalmen start imagining things when they've been alone for too long – poor Adam. Despite all the hilarity the whole group sought to be fine signalmen, and promoted a thorough knowledge of the job and good practice throughout. There was not one 'signaller induced' incident attributed to my bunch of mates the whole time I spent on the Cotswold line.

The balance of company and solitude was not tipped though; there was a quiet evening lull from about 9.20 pm until the last down train just before midnight. I always enjoyed this peaceful gap alone, usually settling down in the chair, as after the final train cleared it was a case of straight home to bed. It is this peaceful aspect of the job I will remember for years to come, along with the distinctive aroma of the 'box. Although one signalman frequently tried, the smell of 50 years of musty tobacco smoke refused to leave the building, certainly adding to its character! However the large, creaky 'box was not always cosy, and on one or two dark and stormy nights I was quite pleased to send the closing signal (7-5-5) immediately the last down had cleared Norton Jct. and leave the place promptly.

In later years another train was added, by extending the 10pm terminator at Moreton-in-Marsh down to Worcester, returning to Moreton and then empty back to Oxford, and the lull was removed.

As I mentioned earlier, having passed out for my first signalbox the real learning then began. I had learnt a great deal from older men's cautionary tales, and here I learnt from my own.

One such experience, from which I learnt to always err on the side of caution, was a case of coincidence, rather than negligence, but still the mark left on me was indelible. A splendid old driver passed to me a note from his guard with the usual token exchange. It was to advise that there was a rail joint which might require attention at Honeybourne. It was stressed that there was nothing to worry about, and as the guard was an experienced ex p-way man, nobody would have any reason to doubt the authenticity of the diagnosis. Not I anyway. The report was noted down in 'the book' - the train register -in the usual way, and as I chanced to know that the p-way gang were working in the Honeybourne vicinity that day, I would report the matter on their first 'phone call. Nothing much else happened, except that two trains passed uneventfully through Honeybourne station, non-stop at anything up to 75mph.

When the original crew returned with a stopping train in the up direction the guard went up to the front driving cab to take down the precise location so that he could notify the trackmen who were lunching in the station yard. However, both driver and guard spotted that there was something far more sinister to be found this time. As well as making the mandatory emergency call to me, they fetched the p-way supervisor Martin Eldridge, whom they both knew, from his lunch and took him to the trouble spot. (Whilst not formally part of their duties, this serves as an illustration of their attitude as dedicated railwaymen.) Mr. Eldridge instantly closed the line to further traffic. The rail end had fractured clean off and landed several feet away in a bush. Having made my report to the controller and passed on the details to my relief I made for home just before 2pm.

The next day things were running reasonably smoothly, the rail had been repaired, and I had a trainee with me in the 'box, despite my limited time in the post. Then a very irate Mr. Lloyd called from Worcester to ask me what had happened the day before. "You had a broken rail, and you allowed the train to go all the way to Malvern and back before doing anything about it...." came the verdict, before I had even completed the explanation. The penny dropped and suddenly the predicament I found myself in was impossible. I either hung myself by agreeing with the accusation or I showed him the note, explaining that no such report was initially received – and incriminated my friendly colleague, the driver. And whilst all this arguing went up and down the telephone I was supposedly running trains and supervising a less than enthusiastic learner. I went home thoroughly disillusioned. Thankfully, the next day brought about a satisfactory ending. Mr. Lloyd accepted that the original report had had no cause for concern or urgency attached to it, and that no mention of a break featured. The driver's manager had tried cross examining the other parties but they proved to be made of strong stuff, and didn't stray from the facts. The rail must have deteriorated rapidly between the two reports. Either that, or two long serving, good railway men had been completely mistaken, made a false statement and a high speed train had miraculously glided over a vast expanse of missing rail – twice.

From then on, every report I received as a signalman was treated as potentially hazardous. This made me unpopular more than once with the powers that be, but it seems that common sense must be dispensed with in this world of blame culture.

The next story follows from the first in contrast. One morning an up train arrived at the 'box with the message that a toddler accompanied by a man wielding a rifle was sighted on the approach to the river bridge. "I expect he's just shooting rabbits" added the driver "but I have to tell you, especially as the little kid was on the track." On clearing back for the train I sent the 'Obstruction Danger' signal (6 bells) to Norton Jct. I informed the controller at Swindon. "I expect he's just shooting rabbits" remarked the man, "caution the next train". "I have stopped all trains for now" I told him, "and I want police assistance, just in case." After the broken rail fiasco I was taking no chances. What if the man was not aiming at rabbits? What if the next train through ended up with a window being shattered, or someone underneath its wheels? Nobody else seemed remotely bothered, but I didn't want to have to explain away a fatality on my shift. I didn't fancy being shot at either, so I locked the door and retired to the chair.

The police were fantastically reluctant to attend, but after 40 minutes two constables turned up. Initially they refused to go along the line because they were without high visibility jackets. They were obviously totally ignorant of what a signalman actually does because they took some persuading that no train would come and run them over without my permission. Eventually a brief search was made and the conclusion from the police was that "they've gone now, but it was probably just rabbits they were after." Normal working was resumed without delay, and I was confident that if any further malfeasance occurred, my conscience was clear.

Of course both these tales were a little out of the ordinary, but the normal day to day work at Evesham was rarely straightforward, not usually for purely signalling reasons but on account of the large mileage the 'box supervised and therefore the increased potential for contingency. The farm crossings created the most problems and indubitably the greatest hazard. During one harvesting season a tractor driver telephoned me from a crossing near Honeybourne, it was very hard to converse with him though due to his very limited English. I repeated "no, wait please" a couple of times, as a there was a down train approaching imminently. He made no acknowledgement but let go of the 'phone without replacing on the hook, so I was able to hear the situation unfold. The gates swung open with a bang and the tractor's engine revved up. At the same time the down approach for Badsey crossing sounded, I knew it to be just a few yards round the curve from the crossing, having walked to it many times for S&T maintenance. My heartbeat must have trebled as I heard the tractor moving off and the train's horn sounding a continuous warning. There was no time to do anything, I waited for the bang. There was no bang, just a "whoosh" as the train passed, then the tractor revved up once more, the gates crashed shut and a voice nonchalantly said "thank you", before replacing the receiver on the hook.

The train driver told me that the farmer had moved up towards the line and waited at a good distance before crossing behind him. I asked the control if there was any chance someone could go out to man the crossing until the crop picking was complete, as a fluent English speaker was needed to properly oversee the movements over the line. The mobile inspector went out until the end of his shift, but after that nobody was available and it was stated that it was the road users' responsibility to cross correctly. It concerned me just how uncertain the whole business was, and that remains the principal reason I was glad to move on from Evesham signalbox. My concerns were proved valid the following year, when fortunately I had moved on. An HST for Paddington hit a minibus full of crop pickers on Poole's crossing, near Charlton, resulting in five deaths. None of the party involved understood English.

Although the additional responsibilities at Evesham could make it a complex job, the signalling work was simple. So when a higher grade vacancy arose at Norton Junction in the summer of 2001, I leapt at the chance of taking on some real signalling of real trains, and leaving behind the nuisance that so many crossings created. I didn't get the job, or even an interview, but I didn't mind too much, I still enjoyed the familiarity of my 'home' signalbox.

Quite a few different specials passed by during my spell there, including some iconic locomotives, such as 'Flying Scotsman' which really drew in the crowds. Many gathered to photograph steam engines as they paused at the 'box and so many Evesham signalmen will feature in enthusiast's photo albums, myself included. I must confess I was very proud to step out onto the crossing boards when 6024 "King Edward I" came through Evesham –the ceremony of token exchange between signalman and engine driver remains, even today, and I was fortunate enough to be part of it.

In the autumn of 2001 the lineside was teaming with fruit of one sort or another. I had been having unexplained difficulties contacting the drivers at the up auxiliary token hut, until it was revealed by one of the chaps that he had been picking blackberries whilst waiting for the down train. Having interrupted his progress I thought it only gentlemanly that I should collect a decent quantity from around the 'box, which I could give to him on his second trip down from Oxford. On his return I gave him the blackberries, and he was very grateful saying that his wife would be very pleased. As it was such a quiet day I continued collecting between trains well into the evening, managing to fill a bucket with blackberries and a bag full of apples. There was only one thing to do with such a crop of course – make jam! With absolutely no culinary skills I set about preparing the fruit into the assortment of saucepans the 'box had to offer. I had a bag of sugar in my locker but it wasn't going to be enough, so I would supplement that from the signalbox supplies. I couldn't believe it when I noticed that the usual sugar, tea and coffee supplies had been replaced with individual sachets for some reason. Undeterred, I set about emptying the contents of hundreds of these little packets into the pot! So for the whole evening's shift, the kitchenette of Evesham (W.R.)'s signalbox became a miniature preserve factory, and to good result surprisingly. However, we had a signalman at Evesham who was obsessive about cleanliness and hygiene (not a bad person to have around actually, as everything was always spotless) so I didn't think he would be too impressed that the wooden spoon and the saucepans were now dyed purple (although I thought I'd get away without reprimand as my mother had provided those). Imagine then the embarrassment when he announced to me days later that he had been cleaning behind the Baby Belling and was astonished to find sticky purple gunge all down the wall. Obviously I had wiped the cooker and any splashes that I could see immediately after production was completed. What I didn't realise was that the oversize lid of the pot had allowed any jam on its underside to fall unnoticed down the gap between the hob and the wall. Hours of boiling, with this constant dripping had meant that rather a large amount of the stuff had accumulated out of sight! I came clean about the jam making enterprise, but he wasn't really the sort of chap who would've been won round with a free jar of 'Railway Embankment Blackberry & Apple Jam'.

Generally, I kept the signalbox very clean though. One job which I undertook daily at Evesham was the cleaning of the expansive floor. Due to all the coming and going it was not easy to keep the floor of the 'box gleaming, especially if the weather was inclement. The ritual of 'putting the broom round' at the end of the early turn (as was customary at most places) frequently turned into a full scale mopping job at Evesham. One afternoon as I had just completed the operation (leaving one dry 'stepping stone' to hop from the register desk to the lever frame there was a tap at the door. "Hello, alright to come up?" called a voice, I assumed it was one of the p-way. "Only if you take your dirty boots off" I replied. "Why's that?" laughed the mystery voice. "Because I've just mopped the whole bloody floor!" I shouted back. After some shuffling, two gentlemen, one in pinstripes and both with shoeless feet ascended the stairs. The shorter of the two briefly introduced himself as being "from Bristol",

and then introduced the suited Scottish gentleman and advised that they were "out on the patch, having a look about today". "Fine – cuppa tea?" I asked, and offered them the usual hospitality afforded to railway visitors in a signalbox. After some informal chat, in which the Scottish chap proudly mentioned that he had started as just a grade two signalman, "like you young man", I thought I'd brave asking what heights he had exactly risen to – as no clues were being offered. "Sorry to sound rude chaps" I ventured "but who exactly are you, I mean what is it that you *do* precisely?" The Bristolian chap chuckled slightly; the Scottish gent looked at me as though I was making some sort of absurd joke. It turned out that one was the Bristol divisional inspector, and the Scotsman - in the tattier of the two chairs, drinking from a chipped mug, and shoeless on my wet floor - was the managing director, high chief of the entire Western region! "Sorry sir" I said "I've not been on long you see…. I thought I'd read your name somewhere?" Turning to his assistant he said "note that down, in future, starters must be given the Railtrack family tree. Ridiculous isn't it - this man doesn't even know who you are!" "Absolutely" nodded the inspector, and turning to me, with a withheld smile "I'll fax you one out."

Later that same year, another vacancy arose at Norton Jct. and this time I was successful. The excitement of moving up a rung blinded me to the fact at the time, but I'm now sure that those early days at Evesham (W.R.), where my dinner was passed over the fence, and the railwaymen truly worked as a team, were the best days.

Alan Gibson, who I worked with at Evesham and Norton Junction. He is pictured here at Machynlleth working the Radio Electronic Token Block system, which now controls trains over the remains of the former Cambrian network. Despite the supposed 'high-tech' approach, the principle is exactly the same as the physical tokens used on the Cotswold line.

The Emperor's New Clothes?

Towards the end of 2006, significant changes were effected to the Evesham token working. Auxiliary instruments were provided on both platforms for the Moreton and the Norton sections, and were positioned in a more convenient location for the short trains we have nowadays. An auxiliary instrument was also installed on the end of the down platform at Moreton-in-Marsh. However, these machines are not 'pure' auxiliary instruments, as detailed in the previous chapter. These instruments are part of their own system between platform and signalbox only, rather than being part of the block signalling instruments.

The method of working is as follows, the signalman removes the token from the block instrument (which they have termed the 'master') in the signalbox as normal, and clears the appropriate signals. Then, instead of delivering the token to the driver in person, he places it in the 'slave' instrument. A token is then free to be removed from the corresponding auxiliary instrument on the platforms. Conversely a driver may enter a token in the platform machine, which the signalman can immediately release from his slave instrument, finally replacing it in the master instrument (to clear the ETT block circuitry) before sending 'Train out of section' (2-1). So, in my estimation the system is more like an 'electric signalman' than an auxiliary token instrument in the true sense – as it merely conveys the token between signalman and driver. I have heard that this method has been used on others regions - but it is not at all 'Great Western' in the purist's mind. The friendlier method, as employed at Norton Junction, consists of a broom handle, with holder on the end, which may be used to pass the token up to the driver's window without undue stretching for either party.

It seemed a little strange at first to have the signals all cleared, and the token still in the instrument, but it makes sense when you grasp that the token is out of the *real* token instrument – but as with all change it will take some getting used to.

As the imbalance of tokens will be severe under the new arrangements the instruments are fitted with transfer magazines. This allows the signalman to lock several tokens into the magazine and then transport them to the platform where they can be deposited into the empty instrument. This does not interfere with the block circuitry, as a traditional token transfer (undertaken by the S&T dept.) does. Several new tokens were fabricated for the new machines, which very disappointingly are not to the original pattern and are an alien design. I think it a little poor to have two shapes of token in use on one system, and the shades of green are contrasting!

And so now each train calling at Evesham, and each down train at Moreton-in-Marsh must exchange their own tokens at the platform machines. At Moreton-in-Marsh this probably speeds things up quite a bit – when waiting for an up train - and also removes the walking from the signalmen's duties. However at Evesham I can't see how the situation has improved really. The pause of half a minute at the 'box has been dispensed with, and now each train takes 2 or 3 minutes longer in the platform as the driver must leave the cab and wander down the platform to fetch his own tokens. Previously he just had to open the cab window. However it *looks* good to the travelling public, as their train doesn't halt yards outside the platform as it has done since 1971.

I'm all in favour of preventing unnecessary delays to trains by small improvements, but am rather cynical about this one – surely the delay is just passed to the station time? I think the effort could have been spent better putting in tokenless block, or better still redoubling the line.....

Perhaps the Evesham (W.R.) signalmen are happy about not going out in all weathers for each train? That was always my favourite feature of the job there!

The auxiliary instruments at Shrub Hill station for the Norton – Evesham section are unaltered and work as described on page 42.

5

Norton Junction

Norton is the first actual junction signalbox remaining on the OWW line. The branch from the MR's Birmingham-Bristol line meets the OWW at 117m. 26c. originally to permit trains from the Midland to access Worcester's joint station – Shrub Hill. The original signal cabin was high on the top of the cutting, overlooking the junction, and 'the old road' – as the MR route is still known today, on account of it being the earliest railway to serve Worcester. Today's signalbox, a handsome GW type 7d, dating from 1908, sits at the bottom of the cutting in which the railway runs, and except for the trains, barely sees, or is seen by anything. The original 3 bar horizontal tappet frame (with 5¼" centres) remains, although sections 1-7 and 27-33 have been removed. 15 levers are in use, two are now spare since the removal of the detonator placing equipment.

The first major change to the signalbox's operation must have been the commissioning of a new phase of Gloucester PSB in March 1969. Norton Junction lost its Absolute Block working to Abbotswood Junction, and became a 'fringe' 'box to the panel. Track Circuit Block regulations are in force on the branch between Norton and Abbotswood junctions. A VDU displays the Gloucester train describer for the local area, and so one can view any approaching trains, whether they are Worcester bound, or otherwise. Trains from Worcester, for the Gloucester direction, have their 4 digit headcode entered into the train describer on approach to Norton Junction, so that the panelman has sufficient time to 'route up' for the train across Abbotswood. The distant signal for Gloucester 126 (Abbotswood) is a motor operated semaphore, beneath Norton's up homes (Nos 9 & 10). As far as I am aware this is the only semaphore signal controlled by a panel 'box on the WR (although Newport (S.Wales) does have a semaphore that is fixed at caution). The branch line is restricted to 50mph and so Norton's

distant signal cannot be cleared for this route. A traditional block bell is also provided for working during failures, and for emergencies. At Norton 'train entering section' (2 beats) is sent on the bell as the train description is 'interposed' on the Gloucester train describer. This is really a courtesy measure to draw the attention of the panelman to his VDU. In the opposite direction it is an invaluable reminder, for trains (mainly bypassing Worcester) 'beep' onto the screen all day and all night, and without the 2 beats on the bell, one could be forgiven for missing a train that is turning left for Norton Junction. The double track TCB line works in almost complete contradiction to traditional block working. As long as the track circuit is clear, a train may be admitted into the section, no permission need be sought. Indeed, on the vast stretches of auto signalling controlled by panel signalboxes, the signals generally remain clear (green) until a track circuit becomes occupied by a train.

The next major alteration was the Cotswold rationalisation, with which we are now all too familiar. Absolute Block working to Pershore was superseded by token working over the newly singled line to Evesham

Right - The traditional wooden steps to the operating floor at Norton Junction. The District Inspector would deliberately stamp his feet a number of times on the bottom step before ascending, so allowing the incumbent signalman time to come to his senses and hide the illicit radio, as well as sending the unofficial bell code '1-2-1', meaning "Inspector approaching - send bell signals according to rule book".

Opposite - 'The Emperor's New Clothes', in situ at Evesham, 2006. Clearly the expense did not stretch to the provision of an additional locker, on which to stand the Network Rail solution to revolutionising the Cotswold Line.

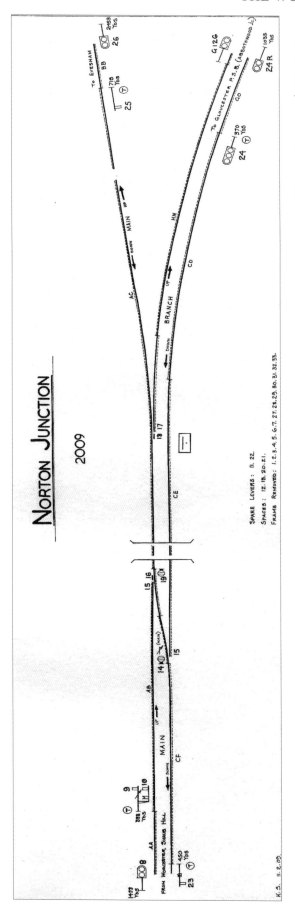

(W.R.). The double junction was removed, and now trains from the Cotswold line must negotiate a 'single lead' junction, made up from the former trailing crossover. This carries a severe speed restriction of 25 mph, although trains onto the Cotswold line can take the junction at 70 mph, and have the up distant (No. 8) cleared to green. In order to prevent trains having to stop at Norton to collect or surrender the single line token, auxiliary token instruments are provided at Worcester Shrub Hill Station. The platform chargeman telephones the signalman prior to each up departure, and if the circumstances permit, withdraws a token for that service (the procedure is the same as that described with the driver worked instruments at Evesham station). He also collects the token from down arrivals and advises by telephone when the token is back in the system, so that 'Train out of section' (2-1) may be sent to Evesham. As traffic dictates, token exchanges can be made at Norton Junction, for example if an up departure is imminent from Worcester, but a down train is occupying the single line, then the token will be taken from that down train, so giving the up train a clear run through Norton. The Evesham signalman advises the drivers whether or not they will carry their token through to Worcester, but being as their speed is low in the down direction, it is possible to show that you intend to collect the token by merely standing outside on the walking boards. Only once did a driver sail straight through, as I was hastily descending the steps. Fortunately, he did the best thing possible to rectify the situation and sped on to Worcester, where the up train was just drawing in, and the chargeman was able to run the token through the instrument and quickly pass it to the up driver.

Up trains may be required to collect their token from the 'box, either when awaiting a down train, or when following another up service. In this instance, the signal controlling entry to the single line (No. 9) is cleared, though the driver is not in possession of the valid token, so special instructions are issued permitting the driver to proceed as far as the signalbox only in order to collect the relevant token, enabling him to proceed. There may be a need to delay a down branch train at the home signal (No.24) in order to safely deliver the token to an up train.

There was a bizarre incident in recent years when I happened to be on duty at Shrub Hill Station. The chargeman had removed the token for a special up train and was proceeding over the footbridge to deliver it to the driver. The driver assumed (as he was running out of course) that he would have to collect his token from Norton Jct, and departed without meeting the chargeman. Obviously, the Shrub Hill signals are in no way connected to the NORTON JCT-EVESHAM token system and so were cleared. The signalman at Norton had also cleared his signals onto the single line in the usual way. It was all easily sorted out when the chargeman spoke to the Norton signalman; the signals were replaced, as was the token, the train was 'cancelled' to Evesham (3-5 on the bell), and re-offered, this time the token being removed at the signalbox to be handed to the approaching train. There was no real problem, and absolutely no danger of a train coming the other way (after all, the token was out and the signals clear), but the authorities panicked. Instead of simply reminding the driver to check with the chargeman before leaving the station, as was the custom, they introduced new local instructions so that the signalman at Norton Jct. may not 'pull off' until it has been confirmed verbally that the driver is in possession of the token. To begin with the driver had to 'phone in, but after this had delayed a few trains, they passed the responsibility to the station staff. As we have also seen at Evesham, the management of the railway are clearly very worried about trains entering the section without the correct token. Whilst in most cases this is obviously quite correct, I fail to appreciate in this instance what is to be gained by supplementing ancient rules - which have served their purpose for decades - with a lot of telephone work, and a lot of running around for the poor chargeman.

Absolute Block working is in force to Worcester Shrub Hill Station, giving three quite different methods of signalling at this little 'box. The bell to Shrub Hill is a flat-topped, round shape which makes a marvellously loud 'clang' when it is rung. Trains for the Evesham direction have the routing code 3-4 added onto the end of the 'Is Line Clear for (description of train)?' signal by the Shrub Hill signalman. Thus an empty stock train (2-2-1) for the Evesham road is 'asked on' by Shrub Hill as 2-2-1-3-4, and the bell continues resonating for several seconds afterwards! The bell to Evesham is commonly called a church bell and makes a bright 'ting'. The bell to Gloucester panel is, I'm told, known as a sheep bell, and makes a deep 'dong' sound. Annunciators are provided on the Up Main, and Down Branch, but (annoyingly) not on the Down Main – where one would be most useful. The branch annunciator made a pathetic buzzing which fizzled out after a few seconds, prompting most new visitors to the 'box to presume that a large bumble bee or similar had just expired on the window sill.

Due to the minimal layout, and lack of signals in the up direction there is little that can be done with up trains, and so regulating for the Cotswolds line is really done in tandem with Shrub Hill. After all, there is no point in them sending an up London train to Norton, if it is then going to stand there for quarter of an hour waiting for the single line, and holding a Gloucester service behind it. Similarly, when regulating down trains, it usually proves best to ask Shrub Hill which train they would prefer first. Towards the end of my time on the patch, a new regulating policy was issued that forced the signalmen to ask the controller which train must run first over the single line if ever anything was delayed. We, the signalmen were told that we could not see the 'bigger picture' - the impact on the whole network. What we could see though were more trains standing at signals with the single line unoccupied, when a chap at his desk elsewhere had ordered "Hold the up!" I suppose there was always good reason for these running orders, but being a traditional area we were more concerned with keeping our passengers on the move than what the 'key performance indicators' were for the network.

However, not all decisions are left to someone else, the actual junction regulating is the sole responsibility of the signalman at Norton Jct. I really enjoyed this aspect of the job, which was so different to any of the Cotswold line boxes. There is an immense satisfaction gained from sneaking a train across the branch and then whipping over the points to pull off the distant signal just in time for a train approaching on the Down Main. It was this sort of work that made one feel like a proper signalman!

The Down Branch home signal (No.24) is a three aspect colour light signal. When the lever is pulled nothing happens instantly. If the starter is then also pulled off then the home clears to show a green – and also its repeater, No.24R (which acts like a distant signal). If for whatever reason the starter cannot be cleared, the signal will remain at red until the approaching train is on the track circuit in rear of the signal for a pre-determined time period, then it will clear to single yellow. This 'approach control' feature is the automatic equivalent of 'checking' the train in, as a colour light signal must not display a green aspect when the signal in advance is at danger. This facility is handy as it keeps things on the move, without the signalman having to continuously watch the diagram – you simply pull the lever and it does the rest itself.

If Shrub Hill Station 'box cleared back after a train had passed the home signal at yellow, you could quickly offer the train on, pull everything off and then give the driver an encouraging wave with the lever cloth so that he needn't dawdle all the way to the starter, which was now clear for his journey. If he was going to be held then 2 or 3 fingers could be displayed to indicate how many minutes the likely wait would be, to save the driver having to get down and use the signal post telephone.

I trained at Norton Junction with my old friend and colleague Alan Gibson, the signalman I had known the longest. I didn't get much training on signalling, (after all I had worked the 'box many times beforehand) but I did get several good lessons in the art of cooking the perfect breakfast, bird spotting, and how to solve cryptic clues in the crossword. They were great days indeed, and actually very valuable training sessions, as Alan never fussed about what I was doing, but quietly observed from behind a newspaper. If I went to do something incorrectly, such as answer the wrong bell, he usually refrained from intervening and then asked "What did you do that for?" sarcastically, after I had received a telling off from the signalman next door! I definitely admired the attitude, as it helped one learn far more quickly, and also helped me in my passing out examination. The inspector who came to put me through the motions was a man from a different area, with no knowledge of the patch, and it seemed, little knowledge of mechanical signalling at all. During the course of the morning he asked me various questions, for which he had the answers written down by an assistant, and he watched me work the 'box. During all the chatter, I got slightly side-tracked from what I was doing and went to pull off for a train that hadn't been offered to the 'box in advance. Mr. Gibson removed his half-moon spectacles and let them fall onto their chain, giving me a "what *are* you doing?" glare just as I rattled the starting lever, which was of course locked. Inwardly I groaned, thinking that was the end of the test, but outwardly I strolled down the frame, offered the train forward and resumed pulling off – the inspector was none the wiser. Whilst not a grave error, I'm sure that if I'd started rushing about in a panic then he'd have suggested that I take a few more days training.

The contrast of working my new post at Norton was tremendous, especially in the busy morning hour, when a train was offered immediately I cleared back for the previous one, and so on. The busyness started with the 6.25 to Cardiff, followed by the 6.24 from Evesham dropping the token off at the 'box. That was quickly replaced so that the first HST to London could depart Shrub Hill at 6.45. Right behind that was another train to Gloucester, and then the return working of the Evesham set, this time all stations to Oxford. This often waited at Norton for the token, as the HST was still in Evesham station. Amidst all this 6M81, a steel train from South Wales to Round Oak would turn up, and wait for a suitable slot to get it inside the yard at Worcester. This also carried a portion for the Metal Box factory. After about 8 o'clock everything settled down, and the job ticked over very nicely. I always enjoyed the afternoon shift, as most down London trains stopped at the 'box and it was a chance to catch up on all the news from the drivers I had known so well at Evesham and Moreton. The service busied up for an early evening peak, and then all went quiet for the night shift.

My first shift at Norton Jct was the night of Sunday 10th February, and my first lot of regular night shifts, and it took a lot of getting used to. After the last London arrival there was nothing scheduled until 6M11, the first freight which came any time between 4 and 5.30 in the morning. For the old hands this was a great shift, with nothing to do – a few even told me to leave No.24 reversed and wait for the first train to wake me up as it trundled by! For me, it was awful, and I remained alert all night with nothing to do, only beginning to feel dozy about the time of the first movements. Eventually I settled into it, but could never really relax, especially as freights thundered up and down the old road all night, and could clearly be heard in the distance. I often thought it would be much better if they actually came via Worcester and then they would be disturbing me for a reason.

One night I got quite a shock though. Just as I had got into the habit of the night turns, and was making the chair comfortable for 4 or 5 hours in it, the door crashed open. In walked a chap I had never seen before with the greeting "alright there, I'm your Pilotman for tonight." I was baffled. Had I instigated Pilot working unconsciously? I then realised that it was nothing to do with me at all. The single line working by pilotman was taking place south of Abbotswood Jct, but it was advantageous to route all south bound trains via Worcester so that they could go straight *down* the up (Birmingham direction) line at Abbotswood without having to reverse through the crossover. It was also a handy place for the

Pilotman to wait and instruct each train to enter his single line. So there followed an interesting night of diversions and all sorts of unusual traffic, and all I wanted to do was have a bit of peace…..That was the problem with nights at Norton Jct – you never knew what you were going to get, so you couldn't really plan accordingly. It goes without saying that any night I arrived particularly weary was always the night that something had gone wrong and night long vigilance was required. Of course, the opposite was true and the vast majority of my night turns there were spent restlessly looking out of the window, stargazing or observing owls and other nightlife.

The shift I hated at Norton was the Saturday day turn, 6am until 6pm. It was a very dull timetable, there was no freight, no timetabled token exchanges at the 'box, no visitors, no one to be seen, and nothing that interested me on the radio – which at that time were actually permitted in WR signalboxes. (Shortly afterwards the management took a U-turn on the decision, and radios became outlawed again.) I believe that was one of the rare times as a signalman that I didn't wish to be in the 'box – not that one anyway.

At Norton Jct, I committed a not uncommon error for the first and only time. A train was passing through the crossover towards Worcester. I had waved to the driver through the open window, as I always did and then waited to see the tail lamp which was present and correct. I tapped out the two bells to the Station 'box and then wandered over to the reversed signal levers. I threw back the down home (No.25) and then turned to write the times in the register. I then went to replace the disc at the crossover (No.19) which I did with quite a slam. As soon as I let go my grip of the lever I knew that it was the wrong one – I had replaced the starter (No.23). I looked up at the board to see the track circuit in rear of the signal still illuminated, and presumed the train would be screeching to a halt. Most signalmen have 'put back' in error once, and now it was my turn, and purely out of complacency. I was furious with myself. However the track circuit cleared and I supposed myself lucky that the driving cab had already passed the clear signal, and my lapse would go unnoticed.

A couple of hours later the same driver came to a stand at my up home, waiting for the down train to come off the single line. When he eventually got the road he drew up to the 'box to collect his token. He was a London driver with whom I was not familiar, and so probably did not traverse the route frequently. "Your section signal…" he said. "Oh dear" I thought, "Now I'm for it!" "You were a bit too smart in putting it back mate" he continued. There was no denying the irregularity, so I apologised and explained that I had made for the disc, and took the wrong lever by mistake. Then suddenly the penny dropped. My forgivable error had led him into a very grave offence indeed. "When did you see the signal go back?" I enquired. "Just as it were level with the cab" he replied "but I won't make a fuss this time." He smiled a smile of

Norton Junction Signalbox, down in the cutting. The original signalbox was on the horizon and the old steps up to it are still discernable on the cutting edge today. Unlike many town signalboxes the windows on the lower floor have not been bricked up as a wartime (and now vandal) precaution. The door at this end leads to the locking room, the battery room is reached from the opposite end. Since this 'box predates the widespread use of relays in interlocking, a separate concrete building, to the right, houses the electrical equipment, as lack of space and dampness renders the locking room unsuitable. The exterior woodwork of the box has now reverted to former WR chocolate and cream, although previously sported sky-blue paint in recognition of two resident signalmen's football teams, Coventry City and Aston Villa.

one who has caught someone out, and then wishes to gloat slightly. I then did exactly the same, adding "it's a good job it was a mistake though, wasn't it." Then his penny dropped. He had failed to stop at a danger signal, which potentially could have been a deliberate attempt to avert a disaster.

I still felt guilty about having been quite lax in the first place, but at least I could be sure that that was certainly the last I would hear of it. Both of us would be much more careful in future with starting signals. I'm convinced the best lessons are always thus learned.

Norton Jct, one ordinary afternoon turn was the first scene of an unprecedented drama. A different driver on a similar turn to that just described, was waiting at Norton to collect the token. When I cleared the home signal and started down the steps I was rather surprised to

see the train approach with no signs of slowing down. The driver was rustling through a stack of newspapers, and as he looked up to see me standing at the lineside, he threw the brake in, rolling past me by a couple of coach lengths. I wandered up the ballast, still wearing my slippers (which were standard footwear in the 'box, but not out of it) to the cab. "Sorry boss", said the driver "just getting these for you" he said handing me a good selection of titles. This particular chap faithfully collected all the papers from the train and then distributed them to the signalman on his return, which I rather appreciated. "No problem" I chuckled, for at least it wasn't raining, and there was nothing else about to delay. We both went on our way, with no harm done. As I returned to the operating floor the box-box 'phone from Evesham was ringing, with an enquiry as to the whereabouts of the train. The man there

The cosy interior of Norton Jct. Signalman Paul Dorney takes a train 'on line' from Worcester for the Evesham direction. The gleaming levers handles and bells are a result of much elbow grease from the resident men. The console on the right is the train describer to/from Gloucester panel which displays the traffic situation on the VDU above. The three incongruous black boxes, which look a bit like car radios, are fault indicators for the Train Protection and Warning System (TPWS). In colour light signalled areas if a TPWS transponder fails then the signal in rear of the failure is held at danger. In semaphore areas no such protection can be afforded, so a fault indicator is provided for the signalman. In one 'box I visited, a decent chap had encased these items in a varnished wooden box, so they were a little more in keeping with their neighbours. At Norton all the home signals are fitted with TPWS, and so is the 25mph permanent speed restriction for Down Main trains over the crossover.

knew it had been waiting with me and was obviously concerned not to have received 'on line' (2 bells) very soon after it was offered. "He's coming now I've got my paper" I joked. "What took him so long?" asked the man, "Well I had a little walk to him" I said, "make sure you're out on the boards in good time when he gets to you!" And there was my big mistake - mentioning anything of it to a third party. Of course I could never have foreseen the farce that was about to unfold, but then that is always the way of things. The Evesham man 'phoned later on to report that the train had passed him uneventfully but that he passed Moreton-in-Marsh without surrendering the token. It later transpired that the driver had handed the signalman there a similar large stack of reading material, and in the conversation had omitted to perform the necessary duties. The signalman realised as he walked away from the train, and fruitlessly looked through the pile of papers hoping to find the token concealed therein – but to no success. He acted quite efficiently in trying to stop the train by rushing back to the 'box to replace the starting signal, but unfortunately it was too late, and so he advised Ascott and the controller. I pondered for a second, and then concluded

that all would end happily as the Ascott signalman could collect the token, parcel it up discreetly and give it to the down train – which he would have held at his starting signal – to convey back to Moreton -in-Marsh. As an old hand once told me "it's not what you do wrong that matters – it's how you get out of it that counts!" The Evesham man agreed that it would all work out fortuitously and that little delay would result, provided there was no further twist to the tale. I was then dumbfounded moments later when the Ascott signalman telephoned to say that the train had sailed straight through and was now proceeding to Oxford, and still in possession of the EVESHAM-MORETON token! "Did he pass your signal at danger then?" I asked, naturally. "No, no, I cleared it for him to stop at the 'box" he replied. That was of course quite permissible, provided the train had been properly 'checked' at the signal prior to exhibiting the red hand signal from the window. Thinking it all through out loud I confirmed that he had been given a decent 'check'. "Well the signal was green, it's only 40 through here so there's plenty of time to stop" he said, totally oblivious to the situation he had created. I didn't quite comprehend to begin with though, so I enquired once more "You did have the distant at caution though, didn't you?" "Err no…it was off" he replied with a tone that began to suggest concern at my questioning. Searching for some credible response I suggested that he had pulled the detonators to attract the attention of the guard, but the poor fellow saw no hint in my line of conversation, concluding that the 'phone had rung as the train passed and so he went to see to that. However the talk then took a turn, as he mentioned that the driver was certainly in the wrong, as the train had not even stopped correctly with me at Norton – the Cotswold grapevine had been working very efficiently that night. The 'phone call had only lasted a minute or two, but I was keen to get off the 'phone, as clearly that signalman would have a bit of explaining to prepare.

The Oxford panelman was called upon to go onto the platform and collect the token that evening, a duty which I don't think he would ever have expected to perform, and it was driven back to Moreton by a mobile inspector. There was much delay and much ado about it all. The next day I was quite sternly told off for having allowed the train to continue from Norton despite the driver's "irregular actions". I explained that I had viewed the whole thing as a misjudgement of braking, rather than a failure to stop and so therefore there really wasn't anything of substance to report. All of my reprimands as a signalman (except the final one) were as a result of failing to land someone else in trouble. And so I shall always remember that evening at Norton, when the token went all the way to Oxford, and all for the sake of an evening paper! Incidentally the Ascott signalman made no attempt to explain his way out of it, and protested his innocence fiercely, and the driver (after a period of absence) returned to the line, still dishing out the papers. How nice that his community spirited nature was not quashed by the ordeal.

Despite the mayhem mentioned, Norton Junction was a very quiet and peaceful place to work usually. There wasn't the 'messing about' with the public and such like, as there was at neighbouring posts. There were also very few 'phone calls, as the delay clerks always bothered Evesham or Worcester, and so it could be a lonely life. I enjoyed the railway work a lot, but I always missed the banter that could found at more sociable locations, especially now I was not working next to my familiar team. Norton was definitely a retirement job, or a stepping stone to somewhere else. In less than six months, I had

read every book of interest on the shelf, and diversified into all sorts of pastimes to occupy the quiet times. We all took pride in the place, so I volunteered to repaint the name plate. It was incredibly difficult keeping a steady hand, whilst leaning so far out of the windows. However it was worth it, as it still looks smart in black and white, and my tiny initials are still in the bottom corner. I liked to keep the 'box clean, but there are only so many surfaces to polish in such a small room, so I began to think about a change. The decision was forced a few weeks later when I had used a dull afternoon to clear some of the lineside vegetation, ruining my uniform trousers in the process. Thinking I had done a splendid job of clearing the banks, thus creating a good view of the car park, and letting some much needed sunshine into the 'box, I awaited my colleagues' approval. Instead I was severely berated by the senior man, for I had unwittingly cut down his precious plum trees! I was not popular with the 'old guard' after that.

The manager who had passed me out for Norton was still in charge, and he didn't seem to mind anybody applying for any old job, regardless of their age or experience, so I thought I might be in with a chance of promotion. I applied for Worcester Tunnel Junction, one grade up from Norton in pay, but far more complex a job. Amazingly I was offered Worcester Shrub Hill Station. It seemed nobody from the patch wanted it, and if I didn't take it, it would be offered to someone from 'off the street'. Daunted by the prospect of jumping up two grades to the biggest 'box on the patch, with less than 3 years under my belt, I thought I'd better go to the Tunnel. "There's far more trains at the Tunnel, of course" said Alan Gibson, who had taken up residence there, "…..and someone else is in for this vacancy". Armed with a false sense of security that the biggest 'box was not the busiest 'box, and scarred by the plum tree business, I took the plunge and agreed to learn the Station.

I went back to work Norton on a couple of occasions after I left residence. It was invaluable to my new job to have worked at Norton Junction, so I was always glad of the experience – it was a lovely signalbox – however I never missed it like I did some, and never returned there afterwards. Passing it on the train recently it still looked charming, with a well stocked garden, and flower baskets, and even Alan's little S&T gnomes were still there.

SEMAPHORES SAVED!

In 1994, a plan was devised to abolish not only Norton Jct signalbox, but also Norton junction. The mainline would become a single line on the formation of the Up Main, all the way to Worcester, and the branch would become a single line in place of the Down Main. Both would run together parallel until Norton where they would diverge, and go their separate ways. However, no physical junction would exist between the two routes, the new junction would actually be the present crossover at Wylds Lane Junction. This was to be controlled from a mini-panel located on the block shelf in Shrub Hill Station 'box. MAS colour light signals were erected to control the approaches. A few sidings and the bay platform (No.3) at Shrub Hill were earmarked for removal in order to simplify the layout, with regard to facing points etc. Token working from Evesham would be extended through to Shrub Hill, which would have been a simple operation owing to the token instruments already being present on the station. The only sensible part of the plan was to enable trains from the Evesham/ Gloucester direction to run straight into the Up Platform line (No.2) at Shrub Hill; this was facilitated by the original lever frame.

The installation relied on the use of 'Solid State Interlocking', a computer processor based system that superseded the use of relays in signalling.

PRIVATE and not for Publication

Signalling NOTICE No. 37

BRITISH RAILWAYS
(WESTERN REGION)
(For the use of Employees only)

Notice to Traincrews, etc.

WORCESTER— CLOSURE OF NORTON JUNCTION SIGNAL BOX

SATURDAY 10 FEBRUARY TO MONDAY 12 FEBRUARY 1990

I suppose it would have been possible in 1994 to timetable the Cotswolds line to function without the junction at Norton, but the branch – or Up & Down Gloucester, as modern parlance would have it termed – just wouldn't be able to cope with the traffic demands when B&G line trains are diverted through Worcester. Since those days, the number of trains on the Evesham route has significantly increased, and may have been unable to do so had this scheme been implemented. So they're probably glad they left things as they were now – the savings in wages would have been instantly spent on delay penalties.

Anyway, the signals were planted, the panel was fitted in its new home, and the closure notices were printed – I have one in front of me as I write. Thank goodness nobody had started to take anything away at Norton, or Shrub Hill as the whole scheme was cancelled at the eleventh hour. I have never been able to ascertain quite why it didn't go ahead, although I did hear that the SSI had strict installation specifications which had not been adhered to, and that there were certain technical issues. But that is not really of interest here, the main thing is that the 'box was left unharmed, and the closure notice was still pinned to the notice board 10 years later gathering dust.

To add further note to this happy ending, the colour light signals (which had 'out of use' hoods on for some time) were removed at a later date, not by unscrewing the bolts into the concrete footings, but by destroying the fixings altogether, rendering the concrete bases useless. "It's downright vandalism what they did with that Norton SSI" my ganger on the S&T remarked, more than once. "That kit can never be used again." What a comforting thought…….

The only visible trace of the Norton resignalling is the portacabin which was to house the SSI equipment adjacent Shrub Hill Station 'box. Today the signalling inspector's provender is held therein, so the installation was not completely pointless – the toilet rolls enjoy dry storage at least!

6

Worcester Shrub Hill Station

Just off the down platform at Worcester's principal station, Shrub Hill, can be found one of the most impressive signalboxes left on the Western Region. The GW type 11 box of 1935, with its bricked up locking room windows and lack of decorative touches (other than those yobbishly applied by spray paint!) is rather drab in comparison to some of its neighbours, but inside lies an 84 lever frame with almost 70 working levers. The 'box was built to replace an Edwardian signalbox on the platform itself, by the title of 'Worcester Joint Station'. The new name was more appropriate after nationalisation, when the station ceased to be truly 'joint'. The role of the 'box at the 'station' end of Shrub Hill would have involved vast amounts of shunting, changing locos, adding a van on here and there, and getting stock in and out of the carriage sidings. A large frame was needed for a small area due to the large numbers of points and disc signals. In those days shunting signals were provided for practically every route, one lever for each signal – unlike today's situation where one disc can often signal a train over two or three different ways. The station had two middle roads through it, which were used to attach and detach vehicles onto through trains on the up and down platform lines, the station 'box controlled the divergence of these lines at the London end of the platforms, as well as the 'Oxford' bay platform and the two station docks. The 1950s local operating

Worcester Shrub Hill Station Signalbox. Note the bracket next to the left hand window, which once carried all the telegraph wires from the 'box. The defunct relay room for the Norton Jct scheme still stands to the left of the 'box. A little cabin standing behind is the district inspector's office, where my interview to become a signalman was conducted. Every Thursday signalmen from all over the patch would gather in the inspector's hut for the 'team brief' which was a monthly opportunity to meet your colleagues, have a decent argument about the best way to run the railway and get a free buffet lunch. Between sessions the signalmen inevitably grouped outside to smoke or chat informally and it was then that the Station 'box man could shout down a request for some leftover sandwiches or cakes to be brought upstairs. Naturally, suitable abuse was usually given back, before any goodies were handed over.

The starting signals at Shrub Hill Jct. Left to right they are: Up Main to (down) Up Main Starting or Down Branch (the route being indicated by the stencil), Down Main to Down Branch with Henwick's distant beneath, To Loco Shed sidings, and Down Main advanced starting with Tunnel Jct's distant beneath. Note the tallest post is for the major route, and the signal to the shed is only a 3' arm indicating that it leads to a non-passenger line, which may already be occupied. Signals structures are surprisingly wobbly when climbed and can move quite a bit in high winds. These signals were featured in the railway press one winter, when gales caused the arms to be blown forward 90 degrees. Usually though WR signals are very robust and so much more handsome than the flimsy offerings of certain other regions.

instructions for Worcester document all sorts of shunting manoeuvres involving gongs rung by code to communicate with the shunters, and 'Vehicle on Line' switches operated by the platform foreman to protect stationary trains before the widespread use of track circuits.

The middle lines both had scissor crossovers to the platform lines, which were signalled by large disc signals in place of traditional semaphores. These were more suitable for use under the station canopy than standard 4 foot arms, and so were used as platform splitting signals. They were also used on brackets reaching out from the canopy to signal the middle lines at Worcester and Gloucester, although in other locations such as Oxford, semaphores were used in similar positions. These large discs and their associated 'calling

on' discs underneath, accounted for 16 of the levers in use. Today only one large disc remains at Worcester, and indeed in Britain, and is known to all railwaymen as "the banjo". It protects the (half) scissors crossing from the Middle siding to the Down Platform line and still has its 'little friend', the calling on disc, nestled beneath it. When I was an S&T apprentice I was charged with replacing the lamp cases on the banjo, which I did, perched on a wobbly step ladder from the platform. I had asked the signalman to pull off gently whilst I was about, but he forgot (or chose to be mischievous?) and whipped the disc over to 45° in a flash. I recoiled from the moving parts and clung to the ironwork of the canopy as the ladder wobbled over. The schoolgirls on the platform giggled and my gang tutted about naughty signalmen undoubtedly through repressed laughter. Still, the photographs of the job went well in my apprenticeship workbook and appear in this work now.

Shrub Hill Station Signalbox, known as 'Station 'box' locally and historically, worked to Worcester Shrub Hill Junction at the opposite end of the platforms, where the middle lines converged back into double track. As well as the main junction for the Worcester and Hereford line from the OWW, Shrub Hill Junction 'box also worked the connections with the south end of the loco sheds, the avoiding line which came from the GW goods yard across to the W&H branch and had the 'Leominster' bay platform and another station dock. There was also the flat crossing over the Hereford 'branch' of the much documented Vinegar line, famously pictured in many books for its queer road crossing which employed railway signals to control road traffic.

The Station 'box worked Absolute Block in the up direction to Wylds Lane Junction, where the goods lines left the mainline and either turned left into the M.R. yard or turned right and bypassed the station on the through goods lines. Wylds Lane 'box was so close to the Station that its up home signal was also Station's up starter signal (No.12 to this day). The rules dictated that trains could only approach this point without acceptance, for shunting purposes only. Through trains awaiting acceptance from Wylds Lane had to do so in the platform, as no clearing point could be guaranteed across the junction. Wylds Lane worked Permissive Block on the goods lines to Worcester Goods Yard 'box, which allowed multiple freight trains to queue up in the section. Goods Yard 'box controlled all the connections from the through lines to the complex of sidings, works and sheds, and the aforementioned avoiding line to Shrub Hill Junction. To the north it worked to Worcester Tunnel Junction on the goods lines, as did Shrub Hill Junction on the mainlines. All this history has been very necessary to appreciate the current installation, because the Station 'box now assumes the duties of all of the Shrub Hill area - once controlled by four separate 'boxes.

By 1967 changes had begun to occur at the junction end. Owing to the triangular nature of Worcester's railway infrastructure it can be easily grasped that trains between Hereford and the North could call at one of the city's stations, but not easily at both. With loco hauled traffic this wouldn't have been possible without running around the carriages, but with the advent of multiple units it would become a simple matter of the driver walking to the other end of the train. Thus a new signal was planted at Shrub Hill Jct at the north end of the up platform, so that trains could depart either towards Birmingham or Hereford. The signal, a single arm with a stencil route indicator displaying 'B'ham' or 'H'frd', still stands today. Some relocking of the Junction 'box frame would have been required, as was the addition of an F.P.L on the main crossover so that trains could cross back onto the correct line. On the Malvern route trains traversed the Up Branch 'wrong line' and regained the Down Main line

The Banjo. Shrub Hill Station's No.80 signal and its associated 'calling on' disc. Now the only remaining example of the under-canopy signals which once adorned Worcester and Gloucester stations. This signal protects what is left of the station scissors crossing. In modern times steam engines are banned from using platform crossovers, however if you look at the platform edge at Shrub Hill beyond 'the banjo' you will clearly see that the edging stones have a curve shaved into them, to allow the buffer beams of larger engines to pass uninhibited.

at Rainbow Hill Jct. Some alterations would therefore have been necessary at the Rainbow Hill end.

By this period interlocking levers had been provided between the Junction and the Station 'boxes to protect shunt moves in the wrong direction. When a loco or empty stock was to be shunted into the Up Platform, or Up Middle line from the Station 'box end, the signalman there would send the 'Working in the wrong direction' bell signal (2-3-3) and if this was permissible the Junction signalman could acknowledge the bell code and reverse his interlocking lever. This would unlock the Station 'box shunt signals (Nos 24 & 27 on the historic diagram, for example). Previously this move would have been permitted but the block instrument being held at TRAIN ON LINE would have been the only protection. The addition of these extra interlocking features was made

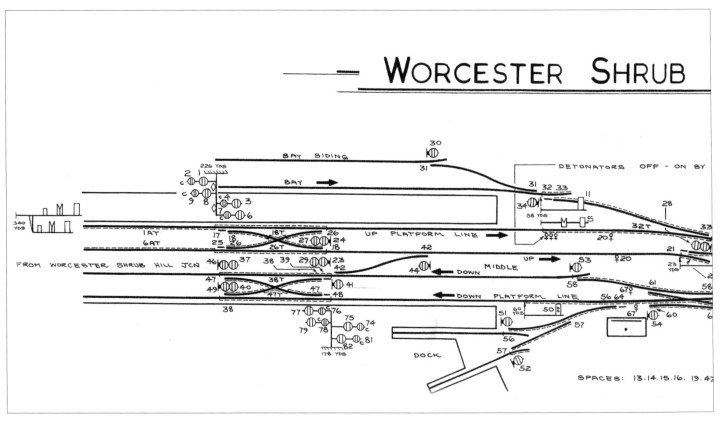

simpler by the removal of the vinegar branch level crossing and the goods yard connections which made several levers redundant in the Junction 'box frame, and able to take on a revised function. A new platform starter (today's No.10) was also added to allow terminating trains to return south from the down platform. These alterations, particularly the bidirectional feature of the Up Branch, could now be considered Phase 1 of the Worcester rationalisation.

The Goods yard 'box was not open continuously and instructions in the appendix made it possible for trains to be admitted to the yard and dealt with by shunter when no signalman was present. The signalbox and its 30 lever frame were abolished on the 18th August 1968, after 64 years service. It rarely features in historical photographs, but its operation would have been most interesting. Connections to and from the through sidings then became hand worked by the shunter, bearing in mind by that era the works had closed and freight traffic was much reduced.

Today, the yard is used by through traffic for regulating purposes or for running round. Occasionally crippled wagons are knocked off in the yard. No marshalling is undertaken and no loading or unloading facilities exist anymore, as the huge goods shed is a retail outlet.

Short signals, with 3 foot arms (appropriate for goods lines) are provided to protect the crossover and connections to the Hereford sidings and North sidings. These are controlled by a 2 lever ground frame and the

shunter simply puts back the signals whilst shunting, and then when the through route is restored, pulls them off again. This arrangement is supervised by the Station' box.

1973 saw the biggest reorganisation in the signalling since the interlocking frame was invented. Shrub Hill Junction signalbox, of 1889 and Wylds Lane signalbox, of 1905 were abolished, along with Rainbow Hill Jct, starting in the September and completed by 18th November.

Wylds Lane Jct is now controlled by the Station 'box, via motor operated points and mechanically operated semaphore signals. A 10 lever ground frame was installed near the site of the old 'box – North Sidings G.F. This works the connections to the Hereford sidings and the North sidings at the Wylds Lane end, and slots certain signals. It is released by interlocking levers in the main signalbox. This is necessary because its connections are inside the area controlled by the main frame. The North siding points are spiked out of use, and the Hereford siding points are never actually used. The Worcester Metal Box company still has a private siding, which saw a daily delivery by train until recent times. However this always entered the North sidings at the centre of the yard, over the hand operated turnouts. When stone trains regularly ran round in the Hereford sidings they often asked to pass the G.F. disc (No.61B on the 'box diagram) at danger to clear their hand points, because none of the shunters had experienced using the G.F. in their training. Few of the signalmen had done so either. During my training I asked one of the older relief men if we could release the G.F. so

I could go and pull the levers about a bit and familiarise myself with its operation. "No bloody way!" he said "we'll never get the bugger back in again…." Despite its total lack of use I knew that the S&T locking fitters still cleaned and oiled it with care.

Another G.F was provided to access the former Midland yard, again released by an interlocking lever in the signalbox. These sidings were removed some time in the 80s and so there is a solitary white lever in the Station 'box. Disc No.68 still has a blank face above it, which was once the G.F. operated signal for the M.R. sidings.

Shrub Hill Junction is now also controlled by motor operated points, or more precisely, hydraulic 'clamplocks'. The Malvern branch is now single track right across the city to Henwick, although it runs parallel with the Birmingham loop line from the site of Rainbow Hill Jct. The entrance to the engine shed was retained and is similar to how it always was. The crossover opposite Shrub Hill Jct 'box was removed and now trains using the 1967 route indicating signal, towards Birmingham run over the Up Main, which is now bi-directionally signalled. The bay platform at the Junction end was removed as were all the middle line connections. The station layout was simplified by the provision of just two through platform lines and one middle road – which cannot be run through other than for shunting moves. The southern end is not too altered as the long refuge siding and bay platforms all remain.

In order to fully utilise the streamlined station, the Down Platform line was made bi-directional in regard to the branch. Trains from Hereford can enter either platform and depart in either direction. Trains on the mainline (that is, to or from Birmingham) can only use the 'correct' line, unless they have performed a reversing manoeuvre in the up platform. The Oxford bay is only signalled for departing passenger moves - none of the dead end lines can be run straight into. The station dock, although facing from the Down Main, doesn't have a signalled move into it from the mainline, but shunt moves can be signalled in from the Up Main or Down (long) siding. Similarly, no train arriving into the Down Platform, in the up direction can run straight into the Middle siding. The route locking prevents this until the train has passed the banjo, and cleared the track circuit through the scissors (CL). Then the 'through move' is completed, and a shunt onto the middle road is allowed. Obviously all that it quite a nuisance is an empty unit from the shed road requires to run straight onto the middle. Usually such empty units come off the shed at the Tunnel Jct end and shunt back into the middle road from the up main. Occasionally it may be necessary to instruct a driver to pass the shed signal (No.24) at danger, with No.29 disc clear, as time wouldn't permit the double shunt mentioned.

So, the current methods of signalling at Worcester Shrub Hill Station are now: Absolute Block to Norton Jct and Tunnel Junction, on the uni-directional down main. 'No Block' on the Through Goods lines to Tunnel Jct, which basically consists of a bell to send the description of the train entering the yard (no permission is needed), and Acceptance Lever Block working (ALB) to

Left - A collar is in place on FPL No. 39, reminding the signalman that these points are currently booked out of use.

Right - The impressive frame at the Station box. The space between the TPWS indicators and the AB instrument (now occupied by the fluffy toy) was once filled by the mini panel which was supposed to replace Norton Jct. When the scheme was cancelled nobody put the block instrument back in the middle of the shelf, creating a bit of extra leg work for the signalman. The lever cloth hangs on No. 31, the crossover from Middle Road to Down Platform line, which has been pulled to allow empty stock to enter the station.

Henwick on the Branch line and Tunnel Jct, on the bi-directional Up and Down Main.

ALB working was developed as an efficient method for signalling short lengths of single line, without the need for a staff or token. The whole section of line is track circuited, which is the primary safeguard for a train in the section. The signalboxes at each end of the single line section have an Acceptance lever, which is painted half red and half brown. When the track circuits are clear one signalman may reverse his acceptance lever, provided he is eligible to accept a train. This not only electrically releases the starting signal of the 'box in rear, but also locks out *his* signal(s) into the section. Once the signalman in rear has cleared his signal, the acceptance lever is electrically maintained in the reverse position, until the train arrives, and the section is proved clear once more. There are no instruments for ALB signalling, the permission is relayed to the 'box in rear by means of a light on the main diagram, marked 'Acceptance given from ......' And so whilst in AB areas the signalman might informally say "peg me up a line", with ALB the phrase was commonly "give us a light mate".

The acceptance lever can also provide other interlocking functions, for example at the Station 'box there are points within the clearing point or overlap (that is the space which must be kept clear before a train can be given permission to enter your section). In Absolute Block signalling the signalman must maintain such points in the correct position once he has given LINE CLEAR to the 'box in rear. In ALB once the lever has been reversed (thus giving permission) any such points are automatically held in place by the interlocking. To reverse the Acceptance lever to Henwick (No.15), points 27 must be reversed, and points 20 must be either normal or reverse. Once the acceptance has been given they cannot be altered.

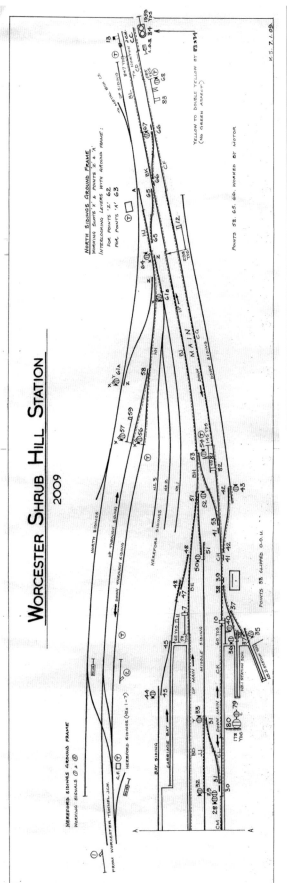

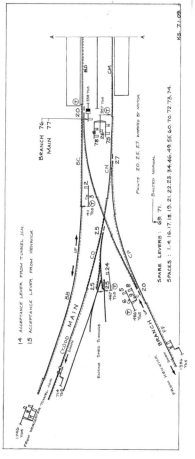

Disc signal No. 35 is one of two Great Western disc signals remaining on the Worcester patch. This signal protects the trap points leaving the now disused station dock siding. The most obvious difference between this and the later Western Region style is the larger disc face on the original example. The arrow denotes which line the signal applies to, and is a Network Rail addition. The GWR expected their drivers' to know every signal for the routes they had signed for, and to which line(s) it applied.

From time to time it may be necessary to cancel a train that has been offered, or change the route of an approaching train. In both these instances an electrical 'timeout' prevents anything happening before an approaching train has definitely come to a stand. To illustrate this principle let us imagine a train has been accepted by Shrub Hill Station from Henwick. Lever 15 is now reversed and points 20 are normal, but it is then decided that the train needs to go in the up platform, which requires points 20 reversed. Provided no signals have been cleared the signalman can wait for the train to approach his home signals (Nos 5&8) and occupy the berth track circuit (FF). Once the train does so, the timeout automatically begins to start its sequence, which is usually 2 minutes for a mainline move. Should the train fail to stop it would occupy the track circuit over the points (CP) which will prevent them being moved anyway. Presuming the train stops correctly and makes no further movement, the timeout finishes and then the electrical locking allows points 20 to be reversed. This 'approach locking' feature normally applies to motorised points too, when the signals have been cleared and then replaced before the passage of a train. Approach locking is provided in the opposite direction as well. If a train is admitted into either platform, via the banjo (No.80) or No.52 disc, the move must remain stationary on the platform track circuit/s (i.e. BD or CM) for 2 minutes before a train can be accepted towards it. This applies to branch trains entering the Up Platform line, when a train has just entered the down platform beyond the banjo signal, because if such a train continued in error it could collide with the branch train on the diamond crossing of Shrub Hill Jct.

To make the matter even more complex, Shrub Hill Station is provided with 'calling on' signals, which can signal a train into a platform already occupied by another train. This is extremely useful to keep things moving (at low speed) in a busy station, and invaluable for attaching/detaching moves. The clearing point enforced by the circuitry at the Station 'box is shorter than normal because if a train is occupying the platform it may still be desirable to accept a train 'over the top' of it. In this instance it is down to the signalman to accept the train by restricted acceptance or 'under the warning'. Instead of acknowledging the bell signal by repetition, the signalman accepts the train by sending 3-5-5 (Restricted acceptance), which the offering signalman acknowledges. Then the man sending the train knows that there is no safety overrun into the station and acts accordingly. At Tunnel Jct this means the signalman checks the train up to his starting signal, clearly intimating to the driver that a steady approach is in order, as laid down in the signalbox special instructions. At Henwick, due to the obliteration of time honoured regulations and the lack of any special orders (that the Tunnel has), the signalman simply pulls off as normal. The 3-5-5 is still sent and acknowledged, the occurrence noted in a different column in the train register, and the person who really needs to know this information -

the driver of the approaching train - is totally oblivious. At the time of writing I now understand that the restricted acceptance arrangements have been totally withdrawn from the rule book, and at the few places that regularly need such provisions the special instructions for the signalbox cater for that. And so one would imagine that they would leave things as they always were – but no! The 3-5-5 bell signal has now been replaced by 2-2-2, which is the old Great Western code for 'Line clear to clearing point only'. Strange that they should reintroduce an obsolete code, and even stranger for a circumstance to which it clearly does not apply.

Worcester is one of the few places where unlimited permissive platform working with passenger trains (and light engines) is still allowed – though not in fog or falling snow. Many other locations have had the practice banned, with the exception of pre-booked moves or notifying the driver beforehand. Where permissive platform working is in operation it is imperative that the signal to start from the platform is replaced immediately the departing train passes it. For this reason, the signalman is permitted by the rules to replace such signals behind the driving cab and not behind the whole train, as is usually the case. At the Station 'box one has to have one's wits about one when the platforms are busy. It is possible for a train to sneak away at the north end unnoticed, and potentially a second train could take the clear signal as being theirs and inadvertently depart into an occupied section. And that is exactly what happened one busy morning when there were several sets of empty coaching stock about the station. The signalman missed the first one to depart correctly for Malvern, and the driver of the second train came out of the cabin to find a green lamp, nice and early in front of his train, and quite rightly jumped in and set off! Fortunately, no harm was done and the second train was halted at Foregate Street, before taking the more usual path, one block section behind the preceding train. What was really required was an annunciator when anything left through the junction, but the engine shed road is the only route provided with such a reminder. Despite such sophisticated safeguards as electrical and mechanical locking, the mechanical signalbox still relies strongly on vigilance.

This ALB method has been about for quite some time, and the WR issued full regulations for signalling by this system. These were dispensed with during a reorganisation of the rules in more recent times of standardisation. The result was that these lines around Worcester are deemed Track Circuit Block because the lines are fully track circuited which maintains protecting signals at danger. However TCB (as at Norton Jct, and on PSB areas) does not typically have semaphore signals, clearing points, full bell signals and the other rituals inherent with Acceptance levers, so all these are covered in the signalbox special instructions. This causes a few problems as TCB regulations do not satisfactorily cover several items common to traditional signalling. For

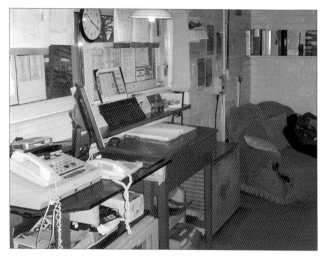

At a busy station such as Worcester, the signalman must liase with several other operating staff. On the back desk are telephones to adjacent boxes, shunters, platform staff and Swindon Control. The most important piece of furniture in view is the signalman's chair!

example, if a train passes on the Down Main without a tail lamp you must send Tunnel Jct 'Train passed without tail lamp' (9 bells). This regulation is very different in the TCB regulations because PSBs can't normally see trains, let alone their tail lamps – the track circuits prove that nothing has been left behind. So if the very same thing were to happen on the Up & Down Main you would be obliged to telephone to advise of the circumstances or falling that send 'Emergency Alarm' (6 bells) which could mean anything. Then the Tunnel Jct man would have no option but to stop the whole job, and all for a missing tail light. This enigma of Acceptance Lever working masquerading as TCB causes significant confusion for signalmen learning the rules and completely baffles the management who dreamt it up in the first place.

There are some special instructions regarding the clearing of signals at the Station 'box. The signalman there may clear his up home signals (Nos 2, 5 or 8) immediately he accepts a train, regardless of the status elsewhere. This is a modern initiative to prevent the signals being passed at danger, and reeks of mitigating damaging statistics rather than sorting out the root of the problem. When a train is accepted 'under the warning' the signal is not cleared, as the calling on signal can only be pulled once the train is occupying the track circuit in rear of the signal, and the regulations stipulate that the train must be "at or nearly at a stand". In those instances the driver is expected to stop accordingly - but he has received forewarning from the signal checks at Tunnel Jct.

Trains not booked to call at Worcester may be offered to Norton Jct as soon as they are accepted from Tunnel Jct. This 'short section' working is permitted because the time between receiving 'Train entering section' (2 bells) from the Tunnel and the train arriving in the platform is very short. Immediately a train is put 'on line' from Norton Jct, the home signal (No.83) and its distant signal (No.84) may be cleared. This is due to the presence of a second distant arm under the home signal, which is fixed at caution thereby indicating that the inner home (No.82) may be at danger. This is useful in keeping things 'rolling in' when trains are running together at tight

intervals. Again, an overlap is enforced for the clearance of No.83; track circuit CH must be clear and the crossover (No.53) must be normal.

The platforms were renumbered sometime after the rationalisation, so today the down platform is number 1 and the up platform is number 2. The London end of both is 'A' and the Birmingham end is 'B'. The bay platform is number 3. 'Train ready to start' plungers are provided on both through platforms, but nowadays the signalman 'pulls off' when departure is imminent. The only attention the platform bells receive is from off duty colleagues attempting to irritate the duty signalman, or by passengers whose curiosity got the better of them and just had to find out "what happens if I press that big brass button?"

One day some naughty person fraudulently pressed one of the bells when I was on duty in the 'box. The bell rang continuously and the little light glowed in the indicator marked 'down platform – down'. I pressed the acknowledging button, but it had failed. I either faced enduring a 12 hour shift with a tingling bell, or breaking a sacred rule by meddling with the S&T equipment. A thin strip of paper in the contacts silenced the thing, until the menders came out, much, much later on.

One of the most frustrating pieces of kit at Shrub Hill Station was the staff barrow crossing. The crossing had probably been there forever, but the signalling for the crossing had gone in after the freight lifts on the platforms had ceased to move. That was in the days when mail, newspapers and other things that people send were sent by rail, and heavily laden trolleys would be taken back and forth across the line. White lights are displayed by the crossing to indicate that no train is approaching, when a train is known to be approaching (by means of the track circuits) the lights are extinguished. For a normal passing train, the barrow crossing works quite independently after the signals have been cleared. But for trains waiting at the signals protecting the crossing, the signalman needs to intervene. By pressing the lock plunger to free the appropriate signal the barrow crossing lights are extinguished and a 45 second timeout is incurred – the assumption being that this is sufficient time for anyone already crossing to clear the line. After this time a comical buzzer sounds, rather like a dying duck, and the electric lock releases the lever so that the signal may be pulled. It sounds rather straightforward, but in the middle of shunting sets about, or quickly throwing levers to and fro 45 seconds is quite a long wait. Even more provoking is the fact that after 'the duck' has quacked, you have half a minute with which to pull off. If you fail to do so the crossing opens itself up again, and the whole procedure has to be repeated. Paradoxically, 30 seconds can be over in a flash when you are busy with something else.

The loco shed sidings have been used for light servicing of diesel multiple units for many years, indeed even in GWR days the streamlined railcars were cared for at Worcester. A shunter is in charge of movements on the shed, from teatime until about 8am every weekday and most of Sunday. A radio system is used between the signalboxes and shed staff to ask permission to 'turn on' a set, or for them to request the shed signal being cleared for shunting purposes. Work with a good shunter was effortless. Work with a difficult shunter could make life awkward. A popular chap in my time at Worcester was Mr. Fish, an old shedmaster with only a few years to go before retirement. He knew everything that could be known about the railway in the vicinity, and worked the shed very efficiently. It is quite limited for space, and there are many sets stored there each night so it is no mean feat to get everything in the right order, in the right place, at the right time, in the minimum number of moves. This particular chap never failed, for many years of experience had taught him well. He always referred to the ancient names for everything, which I liked a lot, such as "the vinegar road" or "the crab", each having its own historic reason for being so termed. However he was not so easily understood across the muffled walkie-talkie, drowned out by the drone of diesel engines. I was the thorn in his side for several weeks when I first began at Worcester. "Tango six AND seven!" he would boom, breaking all radio communication protocols.... "Blossom (as everyone was called!) standin' at y'board, for the station middle... Shirrrrrrrleeeey." The destination typically being sung, like a two-tone horn. "Tango 6. Understood thanks" would come the reply from the signalman at Tunnel Jct. I would be baffled; having only caught half of the details and frantically search the computer screen for a headcode which looked like it might be going to Shirley sometime. After a seconds pause would come "7...Roger that?" "Tango 7 here, umm yes, set for the station middle, um to form the urr?" I would reply, hoping for a prompt. But asking for repetition proved futile. For every time he had to tell you again, he would shout all the louder making it even more incomprehensible, and causing other staff listening in to make suitable silly noises down their radios! After the third attempt, all would go silent. Then the telephone concentrator would chirp, and one of the buttons light up. I always hoped it would be the Tunnel Jct man

who would provide a translation, usually it wasn't, it was the signal post 'phone at No.24. Before I could mutter the words "Worcester Station 'box" he would shout "Bloody 'ell Bloss! Keep up!....Eight O'friggin' eight. Shirley." and trail off into a comment to someone else, about "where do they find these stupid....?" before he had replaced the handset with the exclamation "OUT!"

However, I soon grew to understand Fishy first time, and once I had grasped the intricacies of the timetable it all began to make perfect sense. I always tried my best to accommodate the shunter's requests, after all, it was they who could help you out of a tight spot, just as much as you could help them.

There was one rather stern relief signalman on the Worcester patch who occasionally worked the Station 'box. One night he came to relieve me and just as I was going out of the door, I heard the shed call up for a shunt out into the platform. "Not at the moment" he replied. And there, was his first mistake. Good shunters don't ask for a shunt if they know you've got a train about, and this shunter was a good one. "That HSTs only just gone down, by the time he's done in Foregate, we'll be in and clear for the Brum....and you've got nothing from Norton have you?" Clearly this chap had his finger on the pulse, and was more than aware of the traffic situation. "No, you'll have to wait" said my relief. I halted my descent of the steps, knowing that the reply might be worth listening to. "There's plenty of time mate....." tried the shunter. "I say whether there's time or not" replied the signalman, and thumped the radio down with a flush of authority. "Don't let these guys boss you about Matt - remember who's in charge" he advised, as I bid him goodnight and wandered off to catch my train home.

Every now and again it is necessary to take a unit off the shed at Tunnel Jct and run it mainline to Shrub Hill, only to then put it back on the shed again. These run round moves have to be signalled and booked in the register just like any other train as they are signalled 'over the block'. The next afternoon I flicked back through the train register. That night, no less than 5 such moves took place, equally spaced between 1 and 4am, the only few hours where there are no booked trains at Worcester, and the only opportunity for the signalmen to take a brief nap – or as we said "to study the rulebook!" I cannot pass judgement and say that this was a deliberate attempt to keep the strict signalman from slumber, but I can say that exactly the same thing happened to me one night when the Tunnel Jct signalman tried to take the upper hand with that old shunter.

The Station 'box was in a totally different league to any of the signalboxes I had worked before. There were so many options, so many variables, and so many ways to get yourself in (or out) of a tight spot if you didn't think two moves ahead. Much of the business depended on who you were working next to, in the neighbouring 'boxes – particularly Tunnel Jct – and on the station itself. For example, supposing a train from Malvern to Dorridge was due to reverse in platform 1, but due to a late running London to Hereford it was fortuitous to put the Dorridge over to number 2. What was desirable was a friendly chargeman who could efficiently move the passengers over the footbridge, and a sympathetic mate next door who would take the Dorridge on the Up & Down main (which meant a few more pulls for him), and hold back a Birmingham – Gloucester that he already had on the way from Droitwich. Otherwise it was possible to end up with the Dorridge on the opposite side to all the passengers, and the Gloucester train waiting at the Tunnel's starter, thus blocking the exit for everybody. So you see, teamwork was vital and fortunately I had a good mate in Les Orton at the Tunnel which meant nothing was intentionally slipped in to drop a spanner in the works. Of course it is down to each signalman to decide whether or not a train can be accepted, but when everyone works together, the trains run a lot more smoothly. However, the best piece of advice I was given during my training was "If in doubt you can always refuse a train, but once you've accepted it – you've got to deal with it!" Frequently the Station 'box refuses trains, and invariably because they cannot be accepted at that moment due to other moves (and the acceptance levers physically cannot be reversed) but now and again it is wise to hold back just a moment to see how the situation pans out. If a freight were offered from Tunnel Jct on the Up Main (perhaps 5 'dongs' on the bell, for a 60mph goods) I would acknowledge the 'Is Line Clear for?' signal on the Through Goods line bell (a cow bell which goes 'clunk') to indicate to my mate to put the train into the yard. If I would be able to give the freight a main line run in the next couple of minutes I would refuse the train, and say "keep him rolling" across the radio. One of Station 'box team always bellowed "Rawhide!" in this instance, shortly followed by a chorus of "Rollin' rollin' rollin'!" If by the time the train was arriving outside the tunnel I still hadn't accepted him, then my mate would put him inside anyway and bang out 5 beats on the goods bell. This type of working enabled the use of the telephone (for signalling purposes) to be kept to a minimum, yet everyone knew what was going on.

The challenge of working the 'box was due to the very concentrated centre of the operation. Train crews swapped over at Shrub Hill, units were changed in service, connections were held (often unofficially) as passengers transferred or were taxied from Foregate Street and so there was always something happening out of course. The sections are all so short that a minute's delay really makes a difference. No timetable or control desk could ever accurately plan the busy working of such a small station layout with a tight schedule and so here it is up to the signalmen to think on their feet. I loved this, because other signalboxes, particularly those on the Cotswolds line, had become so stifled with regulating instructions that the signalmen weren't allowed to make any decisions regarding train running at all. At Worcester all the signalmen regulated according to train class, local factors

and traditional common sense. I noticed the controllers certainly seemed to keep a respectful distance from the bigger signalboxes and only intervened when some outside cause made it necessary. There was one, who if I telephoned to notify of some decision I had made, always replied "Good ole' boy!" and that was confirmation enough to carry on. The day to day turning of wheels was left safely in the hands of the men on the ground. I don't know if that's true anymore?

Some were quick to point out that Shrub Hill Station 'box didn't have the highest number of passing trains on the patch, which certainly was true, due to some really decent gaps in the timetable for breakfast and afternoon tea. In fact, if ever I was slow to answer the 'phone, Philip at Henwick would always accuse me of "lying on those lockers again, were you?" But few trains merely passed through Shrub Hill without needing some attention. In the morning the empty stocks coming off the shed fill the station, all three platforms, and the middle and back roads and all depart in quick succession to various destinations from London to Leamington Spa, and Newport to Nottingham. And again at night time the same number of sets all queue up to get back onto the shed, whence they came.

It was during the night shift that some of the hardest 'lever work' took place. I liked to work the layout to its maximum potential by squeezing things in and around one another. Whilst shunting a set back behind disc No.54 to cross over to shed, another inward service could be accepted on the Up Main. Simultaneously a down London could be rolling into platform 1A to terminate. The empty set for the shed could sneak through the middle road scissors after the London had come to rest at the banjo, and then the points could be set behind it, to accept the Malvern empties into 1B under the warning arrangement (3-5-5). It was important to keep a road free for the last Hereford because after you cleared back (2-1) for it, Henwick 'box could send the closing signal (7-5-5) and head for home. On top of it all you had to keep an eye open for the shed driver boarding the units, so you could be prompt in pulling off for him, and then he could go to the shed and trudge back up the platform to begin the cycle over again. And so it continued until about 1am everyday.

It wasn't always easy concentrating through so many repetitive moves late into the night. Once in the dead of night I pulled a disc signal without first pulling over the required points, thus sending the train back whence it had just come! But the shed drivers were a good bunch and could give a quick 'toot' followed by a gesture pointing left or right if they wanted a different road to that which they'd been given. The mechanically worked trailing points at Worcester are not locked by the occupation of track circuits, neither are most of the facing shunt moves, so the signalman needs to take care not to move anything underneath a train. The old rule of not replacing the signal lever until the train has passed clear of

Top left - *Standing near Worcester's famous sauce factory is Down Main inner home (No. 82) with 'Calling On' signal (No. 81) used when Platform 1A is occupied.*

Top right - *Inside one of three relay rooms that provide the electrical interlocking for Shrub Hill Station box. The shelves of the relay rooms on the Worcester District are kept just as polished as the block shelf on the operating floor. In this illustration a monitoring device (on the floor) has been connected to certain relays to record their operation.*

Bottom right - *Up Main Inner Home Signal, No. 7, is one of only two centre-pivoted signals on the Worcester district - the other being at Evesham. The signal has been moved down the post and now takes the space previously occupied by the distant signal for Wylds Lane Junction signal box. This was also of the centre pivot type to avoid fouling the adjacent running lines.*

any relevant pointwork is particularly sensible here, as is a watchful eye on the signalbox diagram and a good view out of the window. Whilst passenger trains benefit from 'fool-proof' interlocking, an empty stock shunting through the station could easily be derailed by a careless or tired signalman.

I learned Shrub Hill Station signalbox as comprehensively as I possibly could, for once I had taken duty there was no going back. At the commencement of my training I really felt like a conductor who was waving his baton up and down, helplessly trying to stay in time with the rest of the orchestra. I would pull off and scribble the time in the register and pause for thought and then another of the five bells would ting, and I would think "What on earth's this now!?" and then I'd recheck the timetable and see that there was something I'd done at the same time yesterday. Or Henwick would ring up and say, "is this train still on refusal, or have you forgotten it?" and I would notice the lever collar that I had placed on the block bell as a reminder that one was waiting in the wings….But sooner or later it became like those first few magical moments on your first bicycle, when you have just lifted your feet from the ground for the first time, and you're off, without looking back. And incidentally, I think it is a little bit like riding a bike, because I went back to the Station 'box once, about three years since I had legitimately worked there. I was thrown the duster and thrown in at the deep end (for I didn't know the new service at all) and jolly well put to work - but it all came flooding back to me as though I'd just been on holiday for a while. "You've not lost the swing of things then" remarked the real signalman.

I did most of my training with Matthew Taylor who was 'Big Matty' and I was 'Little Matty'. Those weeks really were good fun. The vast majority of a signalman's hours are spent alone, but I certainly enjoyed working along with someone else, especially someone as amiable as Mr. Taylor. Later in the year, on certain Sundays, the 'box would have two signalmen rostored, and the duo was reunited. I would do the energetic lever pulling and bell ringing, and Big Matty or whoever else was on, would do the trickier job of booking and working out what to run next, from the comfort of the stool.
The Worcester inspector by this time was Paul Gardner who was more relaxed than his predecessor. He came to pass me out, by watching my conduct very carefully, but without any of the 'grilling' that I had dreaded. And once more, I was back working solo. I was to replace signalman John Badham who was about to retire, having served the railway for 50 years. He warned me to always think ahead to prevent getting "snookered" and to "keep my nose clean" with the management. I hoped I could do as well as he had done anyway.

One day, about 6 weeks into my new post I arrived early for the night shift, to let my mate get off home. There wasn't anything too amiss, but earlier in the evening he had tried to use the calling-on signal, Up Branch to Up Main home (No.6) and it had refused to move, so a fault had been reported. Not long after he had gone a message was spewed from the teleprinter to say that a collision had occurred between a northbound postal train and a car on Dunhamstead AHB crossing. Sadly somebody had taken their own life, which even more unfortunately is not uncommon on railways. Therefore all trains from the ex MR 'old road' could conveniently divert through Worcester and Droitwich. As the news filtered through I mentioned to the shed master that we needed to be smart putting the units on the shed that night as the mainlines may be required all night. But it then transpired that a siding on the shed complex was out of use, meaning that 90% of the sets would have to enter or exit via Tunnel Jct. This might mean sending back trains on the Up & Down Main, or getting them out of the way at Shrub Hill and sending them back on the Down Main when a path was available. The traffic soon started mounting up, as things had begun to start queuing as soon as Gloucester PSB had had to go 'all reds' for the accident.

In the middle of all this my old S&T gang arrived, who had been called out from home to deal with No.6. In order to test the signal they would need FF track circuit 'occupied' and the barrow crossing 'closed', so in between all these trains they were simulating the conditions at the time of failure. It proved to be the electric lever lock that was reluctant to lift, so they came into the 'box to deal with it, and Richard came up to make a brew. "Where are all these trains coming from?" he asked "I've never seen it this busy here!" "Can you spot that tail lamp for me as it goes into the yard?" I asked as I dashed back and forth, for typically, on a night like that a heavy mist had started coming down. The real bottleneck of the diversionary route is the single line between Droitwich and Stroke Works Jct, so no matter how fast I got rid of the through trains to Tunnel Jct they still kept backing up, as did our ordinary sets trying to get back to the shed. Then to make things a bit more interesting the controller advised that they had banking engine problems at Bromsgrove. Any freight that was over a certain tonnage, and needed assistance up the Lickey incline would have to be held back at Worcester – and the Down through Goods line already had 2 long trains on it. I think I dared to put one more behind them, because it was the nuclear flask train formed of only two engines and a wagon. I heard later that evening that there were freights stuck in practically every loop between Bromsgrove and Gloucester. Those first few hours flew by as steel trains, coal traffic, car transporters and travelling post offices passed by, and my colleague sat on the sill of the open window shouting "tail lamp" for each train that passed, and the shunter shouted "just get the bugger on whenever you can" down the radio. After the S&T had finished off and left, the fun continued because the permanent way dept had to take possession of the Down Platform to sort a '36 hour defect' (whatever that means!?) so I did several unusual moves with freight and empty stock trains which

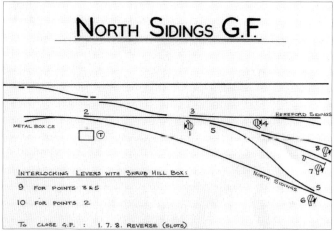

North Sidings G.F. in the 'closed' position. The red signal slot levers are left pulled off so that the main signalbox may control these signals. The blue/brown levers (Nos. 9 & 10) are pulled once a release has been given from the signalman and unlock the other levers for the shunter to use. Ground frame interlocking is often very simple and may consist of no more than bars welded to levers. However this G.F. is a little more sophisticated, but unlike a signalbox where all the interlocking can go under the levers, this frame is at ground level. Therefore all the interlocking is contained behind the frame and is protected from dust and interference by a metal casing.

went through the crossover at Wylds Lane (No.66) and travelled 'bang road' over the Up Main to access the North via the Up & Down Main – this move is not permitted with passenger trains due to the lack of FPLs. I was amazed that the driver of an empty HST for Cardiff did not question the route and happily chugged past the green discs (Nos 68, 54 & 52) spurred on by my wave of the duster and the promise of the route indicator glowing with 'H'Frd' at the other end of the station.

By about one o'clock it had all quietened and the MR line was cleared for the following morning. I must have been very pleased with the whole show that evening, because I wrote all the details down in my notebook, including the fact that I registered 54 trains in the book that night. 34 of those were signalled through between 10pm and just after midnight, and that doesn't include all the additional shunting moves. Now that's what

signalboxes would have been doing every night once upon a time, I thought wistfully. Today, the only lever frames that see such intense traffic on a daily basis are in electro-mechanical 'boxes, such as Stockport.

Someone else's cautionary tales could often provide a useful warning, without having to learn the lesson 'the hard way' and so I was always ready to listen to any, and hopefully take heed. Dave Pagett, the same chap who had first taught me the rules usually had a good story to illustrate each one. He warned me of a 'hole' in the interlocking at Shrub Hill Station 'box, for which I was grateful, because faults in the interlocking were usually only found by someone's error. During my time on the patch, two such failures were uncovered on the Cotswolds line, and both when trainee signalmen were at the controls. As the qualified man sat in the chair waiting to smile and say "you won't get that lever" to the trainee,

Matthew Taylor, the signalman with whom I learnt Shrub Hill Station signalbox is caught by the camera during one of my training turns.

he was surprised to see it come freely sweeping across the frame. Anyway no doubt some similar occurrence had provided the knowledge that the disc to come off the Down Goods (No.56) was not sequentially locked with the Up Main starter (No.13). In most circumstances the interlocking prevents a signal being cleared if the signal next in advance is 'off' – in other words you have to pull off in order. And it was this feature that wasn't fitted to number 56. Mechanical point work is usually fitted with 'back locking' as well, but to make matters less satisfactory, the Wylds Lane Jct points (No.65) are motor worked and therefore rely on the track circuits to keep them from moving underneath a train. No back locking with number 13 is fitted. And so therefore, if a train is waiting on the Down Through Goods to return to Norton Jct, a sensible man will drop a collar on the lever. For if, in forgetfulness, the starter (No.13) is not replaced behind an earlier train, it is quite possible to pull over No.65 points and clear No.56 signal to allow the train to start up the line. But of course the starter will still be clear and the train will go forward into an occupied section. It did happen once, and the 'Train running away in right direction' (4-5-5) had to be used. A simple solution would be the automatic replacement of No.13 signal, but again vigilance is paramount.

Ironically, it was this area of the layout that provided me with my very own cautionary tale to provide the other signalmen with, and the only time as a signalman that I felt things had got a little too close for comfort. I had a trainee (an official one!) working the 'box who was doing very well indeed, and needed no intervention other than the occasional word of advice concerning train regulation. There was a train standing on the Up Goods at signal No.59 and an HST for Hereford on its way from Norton. If a train was not too heavy we often allowed it up to the starter to await acceptance. If it was a long freight it was better to give it a clear run up for the gradient out of Worcester. I was sitting in the chair at the far end of the 'box and generally minding my own business, for as I said the chap learning the job was quite competent. When putting a down freight into the yard the signalmen often pulled both sets of points (Nos 65&66) simultaneously as the short handled levers only needed one hand and little effort. It just so happened that during his learning this signalman had got into the habit of pulling both these levers together and on this occasion did just that, forgetting that only one set (No.65) was required. From my end of the 'box, in the dim light it went unnoticed, until I spotted a signal lever across as well. I knew that all I should be able to glimpse from my seat was a short blue and black lever (No.58) with other things behind it. But instead all I could see was a bright red lever (with a full sized handle) obscuring everything else. Although I couldn't think what was wrong, I knew something was definitely amiss. "What have you got there?" I asked him, whilst standing up and gathering speed towards the far end of the 'box. As I was half way down I realised what had happened, the cleared signal was in fact No.57. This disc was slotted with the North Sidings frame in order to run into the Metal Box Co. via the disused G.F. connections, but it was also the signal to shunt from the Up Goods to the Down Main 'Limit of Shunt' indicator at the end of CD track circuit. As I was pacing towards the relevant levers it went through my mind in a flash that if the driver of the goods took this green disc and moved off we would have no option but to watch him proceed *up* the down line and into the path of the oncoming passenger. Whilst the freight driver might well stop when he realised he was on the wrong the line, the passenger driver would almost certainly assume that white lights coming towards him were on the adjacent line. Whilst he would be slowing for the down home (No.83) there was still the potential for a collision.

Before the thought had passed from one side of

my mind to the other I had thrown the lever back, waited the short 'timeout' and restored the points to their correct position. My trainee suddenly realised what he had done and apologised profusely and went to put the kettle on, leaving me to work the frame. Although the goods train had not moved – I doubt the driver would have been looking down at the disc anyway – the thought alone had been sufficient to remove any complacency from either of us. And it had taught me, and a couple of the other regulars a new possibility, for none of us had ever used that signal for such a shunt before.

Thinking back over the past event, I think it very unlikely that the driver of a train would have taken the disc signal as his authority to proceed off onto the mainline, for train drivers are fully versed in all the signals on all the routes they traverse and are obliged to know the complexities of each station through which they pass. And so that makes my next story all the more incredible, for even now I find it hard to believe that it actually happened – but it really did.

On one Sunday traffic was being diverted through Worcester for planned engineering works on the 'old road'. This happened quite frequently and so made the place quite busy for the day, particularly as on Sundays the direct line between Henwick and Tunnel Jct was closed and so all local trains reversed at Shrub Hill. About mid morning a very long ballast train was offered to me from Norton Jct. The train was bound for Stoke Works in conjunction with the engineering work. As the train approached me, under clear signals throughout, its pace was not much more than that of an asthmatic snail! The train eventually came to a halt at my down advanced starting signal (No.78) with its back end still out beyond the inner home (No.82). I presumed that there must be a crew change taking place, but thought it odd that no relieving driver had telephoned to ask where he should wait, as was the custom. After a while the 'phone did ring, but it was the original driver who requested that I ask the Droitwich signalman to loop him, because he didn't know the diversionary route. Obviously not I thought, because the Down Goods Loop at Droitwich couldn't accommodate such a sizeable train, and even if it could it was forward of the junction where the line diverged to Stoke Works. I told him that there was "no room at the inn" at Droitwich anyway. "Can I go in the yard here then?" he enquired. I became unsure what he had meant by the term "diversionary route", for to begin with I had assumed he meant the Droitwich to Stoke Works section, but now I was beginning to wonder whether the poor chap knew the Worcester district at all. "Well it's going to be rather complicated now that you've passed Wylds Lane" I said, aware that this was a very long train to start back shunting, unsupervised. "Can I continue on at caution then?" asked the driver "is it quite straightforward… signals on the left?" "I can't give you permission to do that I'm afraid, I'm sorry" I replied, because by now I was sure that the driver was totally inexperienced and could

well have been on his first day in the job or something. "I've really dropped a clanger here, haven't I, I'm going to be in a lot of trouble about this" he said, sounding very disheartened. I restrained my honest instinct to answer a hearty "YES" and instead, with a view to getting some traffic on the move suggested "why don't you give me tail lamp, and in the meantime I'll sort something out and we'll get you inside the yard." He did not understand, but because I couldn't see the rear of the train, I could not ascertain it was complete and so therefore could not give 'Train out of section' (2-1) to Norton Junction in order to accept the next train. As the young chap trudged passed my 'box I exchanged a few reassuring words with him, after all it wasn't really his fault he had got into such a mess, it was a lack of decent training, and some bad crew diagramming clearly.

Now, before sectorisation and privatisation all drivers in a particular depot would have known all the various routes, and traction required in that area, but modern organisation confines drivers to select routes and often a particular type of train. The driver manager on duty that day at Worcester was an old hand and came out to see if there was anything he could do to help. He would have remembered the shunt moves all around the locality, despite not having driven a freight train for years. And I dare say he would have been quite competent to have driven the ballast train onto Stoke Works or at least conducted the official driver there, but rules are rules and so the controller said that only a driver from the relevant company could assist, and no such driver could be found. Eventually the mobile inspector arrived to supervise the scene. By now there was a train standing at Shrub Hill Nos 78, 83, & 7, Tunnel Jct's No.6, Henwick's No.5 and Norton Jct's Nos 23, 24 & 25. The driver was by now a nervous wreck, but the inspector had a grin like a Cheshire cat, for he was going to get a footplate ride. I mused that once upon a time trains were back shunted into refuge sidings all over the place, and shunted onto the opposite line to allow something to pass, but nowadays such moves are extremely rare, and even then require someone on the ground to relay hand signals or use a walkie-talkie.

I sent 'Shunt into forward section' (3-3-2) to the Tunnel Jct, and he gave me a LINE CLEAR to allow the ballast train to pull forward sufficiently far enough to clear No.10 signal. Then the train was routed up the main, also needing to pass the advanced starter (No.13) to clear the yard points – which is why the London train was held in the platform and not allowed to proceed towards Norton. On completion of the shunt 8 bells is sent (Shunt withdrawn) and the Tunnel man can replace the block to NORMAL, and reset by winding the time release. Then finally the train was admitted to the yard, by No.67 disc, and the line was clear once more.

Trains were eventually queuing back to Moreton-in-Marsh, Barnt Green, Cheltenham and Ledbury, and the total delay attributed to the event was over 40 hours in the end! I relay this tale, not to humiliate the driver (who I'm convinced suffered enough that day) but to highlight the problems associated with a fragmented industry. Everyone at Worcester that day was willing to cooperate, everyone sought to get the service running again, but no one was allowed to get in the cab and actually shift the train, despite highly experienced men waiting nearby.

Working the Station 'box was enjoyable and challenging, but had the potential to be very frustrating. Units were often abandoned in the platform, due to a driver hours being completed, but rarely did anyone advise you of such and so other things were unnecessarily delayed, especially at night time. Then they changed the signalmen's general instructions so that once a signal was cleared for a move, the signalman was no longer permitted to replace that signal to danger (other than in an emergency) without first confirming the alteration with the driver. So, even if a train was obviously driverless you were stuck until somebody bothered telling you what was going on. Sensibly the regular signalmen avoided clearing any signals for empty sets until a driver contacted to say that they were waiting, but often they didn't make any contact anyway. Then a local directive advised us to 'pull off' according to the timetable and the regulating policy - our job might as well be done by a machine. There is neither finesse, nor efficiency in merely pulling off to schedule, particularly when the circumstances outside suggest that it would be inadvisable. And so I did as I was told, and when anything went wrong I was supposed to report the culprit to the controller immediately – which anyone can understand did nothing to foster good relations. The age old rivalry between driver and signalman was resurrected.

One day I had a usual move of a Birmingham to Malvern service reversing in the up platform (2B) and a Malvern to Birmingham service turning in the down platform (1B). The Malvern came in later than expected, but the Birmingham was in and ready to depart right time.

Now under these circumstances no one, without the aid of a crystal ball, can adequately predict what the best course of action is, but following my orders I cleared the down starter (No. 78) for that train was right time. Had I given priority to the Malvern train then typically the crew would have taken their scheduled five minutes to change ends (which they often did, regardless of late running) and another delay would have been caused. But the law of Murphy can always be relied upon, for on that day the late running crew swapped over in record time, and seeing *a* signal clear (for the adjacent line) proceeded passed the platform starter (No.76/77) at danger and were brought to an abrupt halt by the Train Protection and Warning System (TPWS). I replaced No.78 to danger and sent 6 bells to Tunnel Jct – the emergency alarm, under TCB regulations. The whole thing was dealt with smartly, little delay occurred and I thought no more of it. One of my colleagues mentioned the regulating decision, and added "of course if you'd run it in the first place, the Brum could have had the SPAD – you can't win" and he was of course absolutely correct.

About two weeks later, on the first morning back after Christmas, I was faced with a very similar situation. There was a stopping train which had been late into platform 2, despite the 'timetabled' clearance of signals as prescribed. No driver had made contact and control were advised as directed. There was also a right time train in platform 1, of a higher priority, so I signalled the Class 1 train out. To my amazement the train in platform 2 moved off instead. Again, it was all tidied up quite rapidly and apart from the incredible coincidence of lightning striking twice in the same place, I thought no more about it. However the gremlins that had caused two drivers to misread the same signals still had a lot more havoc to wreak, for that was not to be the last I heard of the matter. It was to be the beginning of the end for me.

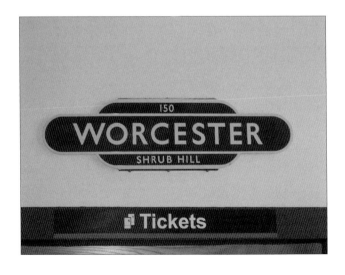

7

Worcester Tunnel Junction

Forty-one chains from Worcester Shrub Hill Station 'box and almost 121 miles from London, lies Worcester Tunnel Junction signalbox or 'The Tunnel'. That extra chain makes all the difference because blockposts which are less than half a mile apart must abide by stricter regulations concerning acceptances during fog and such like – fortunately none of them concern us here thanks to those 22 yards. The junction is so named because the 212 yard Rainbow Hill tunnel commences just to the north. The 'box sits in the deep cutting, along which Railway Walk runs atop. Many a spotter viewed the loco shed from this vantage point, and many published photographs bear testament to this fact. You can still see the 'box and the shed sidings from the path today, although you will have to peep through lots of vegetation, which nobody bothers clearing away nowadays. Unfortunately as well as train spotters certain undesirables use this path and so the rear of the 'box has mesh fitted to its windows and a shipping container provides refuge for the signalman's car.

As well as vandals the 'box has suffered from another problem – trains! The south end of the 'box has clearly been rebuilt as a result of a train running into it in the '70s, which is not too surprising due to the position of the shed exit road buffers. At the end of the '90s a train struck the buffers once more, but this time the train fared worse than the stops. The mangled mini plough that had been fitted to the class 150 'Sprinter' unit lay in the signalbox coal bunker for months as a stark reminder to the unfortunate driver who reportedly misread the Down Main home signal (No.17) instead of the shed exit signal (No.39).

The 'box is a type 7, dating from 1905 and the current frame of 58 levers has been reduced in size from the 77 which were fitted in 1960. The GW vertical tappet 5 bar frame, with the levers at 4" centres was installed to

The south end of Worcester Tunnel Junction signal box showing the variation in the colour of the brickwork, the result of a train failing to stop at the buffers seen in the foreground. In years previous, Railway Walk, at the top of the bank on the left, was a favourite spot for views of the steam shed at Worcester.

Having cleared the signals for a train to enter Foregate Street Station , signalman John Price checks the progress of approaching trains on the 'TRUST' computer. Behind the frame three wire adjusters can be seen. These are used to counter-act expansion and contraction ensuring the signal shows 'a good off'. They are invaluable, particularly in summer weather.

Weetabix for breakfast.

For many years the 'box had no telephone concentrator and so there was one telephone on the shelf for each one outside. When the S&T tested the phones you could see the signalman walking the length of the frame picking up each receiver until a voice replied on the correct one. The box to box phones were hung on the back wall beside the train register desk and when they sounded the signalman would often pick up both and hold one to each ear before replacing the one that had nobody on the other end. A couple of years ago this routine was abolished when a telephone 'concentrator' with flashing lights and buzzers took over.

This signalbox would certainly have been the busiest in all the district, in its heyday, as all the routes north converged here. Today it is still very much 'on the go' all day and with the shunt moves, on and off the shed through the night, the stream of traffic is pretty constant across the 24 hours. Although the goods connections are much thinned out, the layout is basically similar to the original. During the resignalling the bidirectional facility from Shrub Hill's up platform was extended to The Tunnel, and the line near the site of Rainbow Hill Jct became single, but otherwise it has an 'intact' feel about it, and is lacking in many of the mod-cons fitted in the other 'boxes we have seen. One throwback to the old days is the shunters' warning lights which warn when a train has been signalled through the tunnel, although the days of shunters clambering about under stock, on or near main lines is pretty much over now, thanks to the DMUs with their automatic couplings operated by push-buttons in the cab.

Another remnant of the past is lever No.27 which formerly controlled the points into the carriage siding adjacent the Up Droitwich Loop line. These also acted as a throw off to anything rolling back towards Rainbow Hill Jct. The siding is gone, but the lever remains and must be reversed before a train can be signalled up the loop. Levers 'worked to maintain interlocking' are an economy measure when the layout is changed but the locking is not altered accordingly. They are getting more and more common on the modern railway, but this is the only one at Worcester, as most of the alterations pre-date 'cheap and nasty' solutions.

You may notice that the Droitwich Loop line is 'up' to Droitwich Spa, but then joins the Down Main at Tunnel Jct. Such trains are booked on the down page of the register but 'D/L' or a similar note is made in the 'line' column. Similarly, up trains going to Henwick are entered on the up page, but suitably marked. Trains booked into the yard are described from Droitwich with the 3-4 (turning left) suffix, trains for the loop line have a 1-5 (turning right) suffix added. Tunnel Jct provides the same service for the Droitwich man by adding 1-5 to the description of any train that is for the Bromsgrove direction. Many trains terminate in Foregate Street station (platform 2) and don't actually continue through to Henwick. They are in effect a shunt move, in rear of

replace a double twist frame of 65 levers. Unlike most of the WR frames the running signals are all bunched up at the left hand end of the frame, rather than at the extremes, or in later cases (such as Evesham WR) the middle. As much of the pointwork has now gone and the redundant levers removed, the frame has a lop-sided appearance with a large gap between No.39 and the remaining points No.s 56/57. However the man on duty still has plenty of walking to do because the instruments are rather spread along the shelf and the Up & Down Main bell to The Station is unhelpfully located some distance from the relevant acceptance lever. The points to come out of the yard illustrate very well the principle that technique is more important than strength when it comes to levers. They would come across no bother, but getting them back was a different kettle of fish – I never really found the knack and needed to make two attempts. Many a Monday morning fault for the Worcester S&T was "58 points, hard to normal" and many a fault was remedied with a drop of oil, and the conclusion that the signalman needed more

Tunnel Jct's home signal (No.20) and so these are signalled to Henwick as 5-2 (reverse acceptance lever for shunt move). Once the train returns on its Birmingham working 2-5 (shunt complete) can be sent to Henwick and the acceptance lever is restored. Problems were experienced with this move as the station foreman bells the trains in and out of the platform to Henwick signalbox. However, when the platform bell sounds, the man in the 'box can't be sure if that means the train has just closed its doors, if it is at a stand at the signal or anywhere in between, as GN is one long track circuit. Eventually, to reduce all this guess work a treadle was fitted on the approach to the signal, so the Tunnel man can be sure he is pulling off for a train that is actually waiting there when the audible warning sounds.

On the way down the Droitwich Loop drivers encounter a 'banner repeater signal (No.8R). Due to the curvature of the line, the required sighting distance for the starter signal (No.8) is not possible so the repeater warns drivers to the state of the signal in advance. For as long as anyone can remember, this was an electro-mechanical device in a glass fronted case lit by paraffin lamp. For some reason it was replaced in 1999 by an electric lamp working through fibre optics. Not only was this new signal 'upper quadrant' (quite out of place at Worcester) it seems nobody had considered what would happen in the event of a mains power failure. If the banner goes out altogether than the circuitry proving that signal No.8 is 'on' is incomplete and consequently the acceptance to Henwick cannot be given and working by Pilotman must be brought in - there's progress for you. Incidentally, not far from this signal, by the site of the old Goods engine shed are two large air-raid shelters in the ground which protected the shed staff from Hitler's bombs, not that the signalman would have benefited from this protection though, they would have diligently remained at their post to see to any trains.

Another little peculiarity is that the Up Main starter (No.6) is motorized and replaces itself to danger when a train passes it. This feature is useful for such a short section although I can't really understand why it wasn't fitted in the opposite direction (to Shrub Hill

The interior of 'The Tunnel' with its depleted frame, but busy block shelf. The different shape block-bells producing different tones are evident.

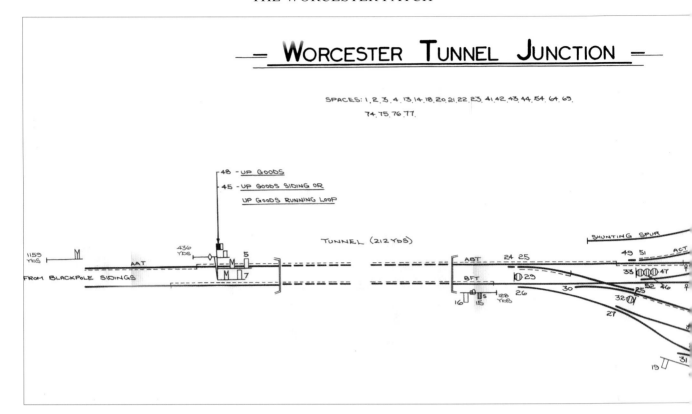

Station's No.77) where the likelihood of a train following another into section is much increased.

Trains heading north from Shrub Hill are offered to Droitwich immediately they are accepted (if conditions permit) as the section is so short. One they are put 'on line' (2 beats) from the Station they are probably directly on the approach to the home signal (No.s 17 or 18). In fact unless the signalman is quick in responding, the block instrument will automatically swing to TRAIN ON LINE by the occupation of DD track circuit. The signalman must be very aware of his clearing points here. The line must be clear for a quarter mile ahead of the home signal (No.17) to accept on the Down Main, and the crossover (No. 36) must be reversed to accept on the Up & Down Main. Obviously at a busy spot there can be several trains wanting an overlap across the junction, so judicious use of the reminder appliances is wise. There is a flap on the block instrument that can be swung across, preventing LINE CLEAR from being given and revealing the engraving CLEARING POINT FOULED.

I was never 'passed out' for the Tunnel 'box, although as a Shrub Hill man I was familiar with its workings as the two 'boxes had to do pretty much everything in cooperation. Either 'box could make life difficult for the other, for example, if an up train is allowed through to wait at the starting signal (No.6) that removes any possibility of a train leaving the up platform (2A) at Shrub Hill to go down. Similarly, if trains for Shrub Hill are queuing up, the Tunnel can be left with something hanging over the junction, blocking anything in and out of Foregate Street. A little give and take makes for

smoother operation all round. I had a few turns on the frame at Tunnel Jct with Alan Gibson who had moved there from Norton Jct shortly before me. I always found it a very satisfying job indeed with plenty of action and plenty of split second decisions for regulating. The big downside was that due to the shed working the 'box had some very unsociable duties. It opens at 6am on a Sunday whilst all the other signalmen are in bed and it even has a night turn on Boxing Day, so the shunters may sort everything out after the two day closedown. And of course, every night the trains are moving about under the floodlights outside being washed, fuelled and cleaned for another day's service. In order to move from one siding to another on shed the trains pass the shed signal (No.39) and 'Shunt into forward section' towards Droitwich. The bellcode 3-3-2 is sent, and Droitwich pegs TRAIN ON LINE, then the train is admitted via the subsidiary 'shunt ahead' arm (No.15). This tells the driver he may proceed into section but only as far as is necessary for the shunt move. As this is a regular move a track circuit (DH) is provided in the tunnel. When all is back in the confines of the station limits 'Shunt withdrawn' (8 bells) may be sent to Droitwich and the block returned to NORMAL. Rather than doing this throughout the night, it is normal practice to request the shunt at the beginning of shunting moves and leave it on until shunting is finished in the morning. This allows both signalmen some peace and quiet through the night. One particular chap at the Tunnel was well known for nodding off (and not just in the small hours) but there was no getting away with it there, for the shed

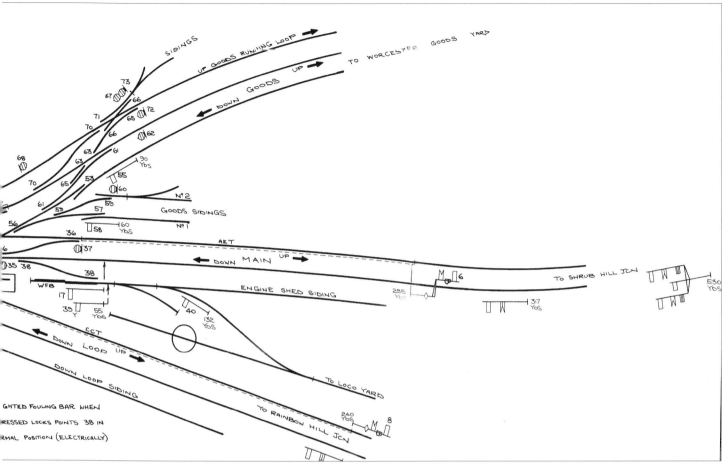

foreman could very easily stomp up the 'box steps and hammer on the door!

Being a little remote from the hub of the station, the Tunnel is a bit of a hideaway from prying eyes and unnecessary interruptions, but still a busy number that requires very decent signalmen. My memory of the dimly lit place is that it was always filthy, as shed 'boxes tended to be, although without the excuse of smoke and soot anymore. The lever tops were red with rust as the men considered it too busy to mess about with lever cloths and polishing. The main resident man for years was Colin Jones who made splendid railway tea with leaves, so that the last few mouthfuls were always a bit chewy. Cigarette smoke filled the 'box to choking point, but there was always a friendly bark to 'come on up' and he was very pleased to explain the workings of the place, utilising the broom to point ferociously to things on the diagram – I was amazed that the glass never cracked! Colin was one of the first signalmen I met - during my week away from school I was taken to visit the 'box – and one of the last, for he used to walk along the boards in front of Shrub Hill on his way to work, and always shouted up as he passed. However, all eras come to an end and nowadays the place is spick and span and even has flower baskets outside. Whilst cleanliness is to be applauded I suppose, I can't help but feel that the evocative spirit of the dirty old Tunnel 'box has somehow been wiped away along with the dirt and grime.

The Tunnel has had more than its fair share of mishaps throughout the years, other than those already mentioned concerning the infamous buffer stops. During a block failure in the first few days of 1974 'time interval working' (which is no longer permitted) was in force and a train from Droitwich smashed into the rear of another train resulting in the death of the enginemen. The accident report of this incident is publicly available for those interested. In this decade a train also ran through the section when another train was already occupying it, although fortunately the first had come within the protection of the home signals before the second's arrival. Perhaps the most unusual was due to an S&T failure and a hasty signalman. When I was an S&T apprentice Mr. Finch showed me a photograph of a first generation DMU on the Droitwich Loop, with the passengers being helped down and processing back along the cess. "What's happened there then?" he asked. I looked for a second and then realised that the train was on both roads. The second coach was straddling the up *and* the down loop lines. The signalman had been too quick in putting back the signal and reversing No.37 points and a gaping hole in the electric interlocking, caused by a fault, had allowed the points to motor over with a train standing on them. Questions must have been asked all round I imagine.

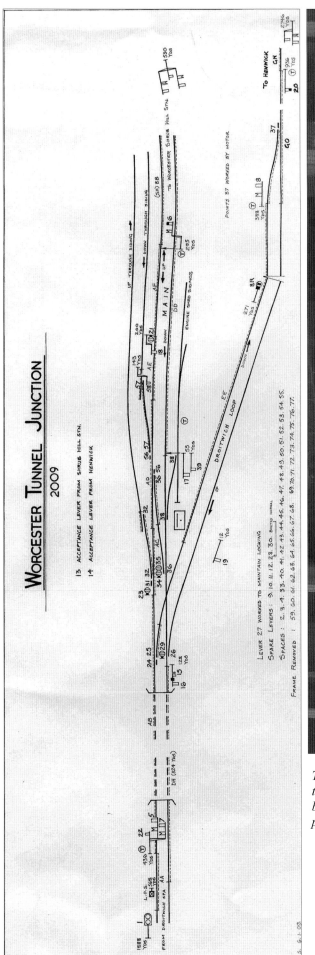

The rear of Worcester Tunnel Junction Signalbox. The back of this 'box is more interesting than most, due to the chimney still being in place and the unusual brackets securing the cast name plate centrally either side of the chimney breast.

8

Droitwich Spa

At 46 feet long, Droitwich Spa Signalbox is the biggest and most northerly of the Worcester patch. There was an earlier 'box at Droitwich built at a similar time to the other early signalboxes on the route, but the large type 7d of today replaced it in April 1907. The 79 lever frame remains, although the 3 bar horizontal tappet interlocking has been converted to the 5 bar vertical system. The levers, with their 5 ¼ inch spacing, mean the frame still fills the generously proportioned building.

The layout outside is rather interesting. It can be seen in the 1935 diagram that the down line was fitted with 'splitting homes' and 'splitting distants' – that is to say the lie of the junction was indicated to the driver well in advance. The WR practice, other than at very high speed junctions, was to have a single distant signal which only cleared for the main route, as diverging trains would need to slow anyway. The signal protecting the actual junction shows which route is set but signals in rear usually do not. Thus at Droitwich today the junction signal on the end of the Birmingham platform signals trains either Down Main or Down Goods Loop and the next, much taller bracket, indicates whether the train is signalled mainline (Hartlebury) or branch (to Stokeworks). This accounts for some of the white levers at the left hand of the frame. There was once a middle siding on both the main and branch lines, and although both have gone the signal which once protected the exit from the main middle road (No.15) remains and is useful when trains are queuing signal to signal. The Down Main advanced starter (No.16) was a particularly heavy pull and during my stint with the S&T, was converted to motor operation. On the up road there have been some substantial changes, as the Up siding, or Berry Hill siding was converted into a goods loop. In order to make some room the up line detonator placers became worked by a small 2 lever frame with the legend 'McKenzie and Holland – Worcester' cast on the side. The levers that became spare as a result enabled the new goods loop signals to be worked from the appropriate place in the frame. The up sidings, between the junction and the station, served a coal merchant and survived the Beeching era. There was even a resident shunting engine stabled there until the 1980s, but all had gone by the time I made acquaintance with the area. Again, although the middle siding has gone the associated signal on the Up Main remains and so Droitwich boasts an impressive 5 running signals on each mainline.

I remember one day our S&T gang were called to the Up Main motor worked home signal (No.75) as something was amiss. A maintenance gang, normally assigned to the MAS lines around Bromsgrove had just been working in that area, so as you can imagine all sorts of aspersions were cast en route. Signal motors have a small brake shoe which holds the arm in the 'off' position. Once this brake is released, either intentionally or due to its 'fail-safe' design, the arm automatically returns to the danger position. During some liberal oiling of the motor's innards the brake shoe had been accidentally covered in oil. The result was that the signal would motor 'off', return to 'on' and then repeat the cycle as the circuitry was still 'asking' the signal to clear. When we arrived the arm was going repeatedly up and down, until a quick wipe round with a rag restored order. Fortunately no trains arrived whilst the 'flashing aspect' was being displayed.

The Up Main distant signal (No.77) is now very special, as it is the only working semaphore distant signal on the patch (remembering that the arm underneath Norton Jct's home belongs to Gloucester). As it is a single arm on its own post it has a yellow finial ball, which must be extremely rare on the WR, who systematically installed colour light distant signals throughout the 1950s. Semaphore distant signals do create slight problems in fog or falling snow as their visibility cannot compare with a colour light signal, although of course the AWS magnet does assist by giving the driver an audible warning of its position. The normal rulebook requirements for these circumstances is that a train may not be accepted from the box in rear until the section to the advance is empty. In view of all the stop signals at Droitwich and the great distance between the distant and the actual signal leading into the next section, these strict rules are relaxed by way of a special instruction.

The branch line to the Midland has seen the most alteration and was resignalled in connection with the opening of Gloucester panel. The line is now single from Droitwich until it meets the MR mainline at Stokeworks Jct, south of Bromsgrove. The line is regulated by the Track Circuit Block rules and in practise is very similar to the single line between Ascott-under-Wychwood and Oxford, with the big difference being that it is Droitwich that has control of acceptance, not the panel signalman. The train descriptions are sent and received on an ordinary single stroke bell, and when a train is to be signalled from Stoke Works the Droitwich man reverses his interlocking lever (No.19) to give the 'slot' to Gloucester PSB. (This lever is blue and brown, and although it does give acceptance, it should not be confused with the red and brown acceptance levers used at Worcester which have evolved from a different system to that used here.) In order to reverse this lever all the appropriate track circuits must first be proved clear and points 13 must be in the normal position. When a train enters the single line an annunciator automatically sounds in the 'box. When a

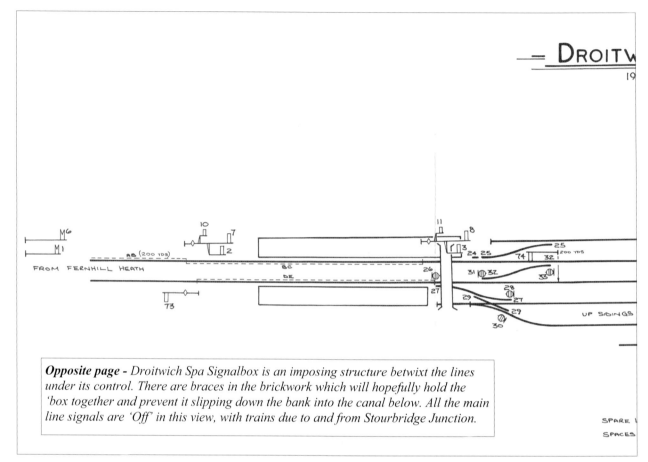

— DROITW

From Fernhill Heath

down train is sent to Stoke Works lever 13 is locked in the reverse position until the branch line becomes clear once more. This ensures that anything rolling back towards Droitwich would be thrown off at the trap points, in advance of the Up Branch home signal (No.78). Unusually for a colour light signal there is no AWS magnet fitted to the Down Branch starter (No.12) and so trains, which will have received a warning indication at the Down Main distant (No.6) retain the yellow 'sunflower' indication in the cab all the way to Stoke Works Jct. In semaphore areas the AWS is really only of value for the distant signals – for which it was first developed by the GWR.

Theoretically the signalbox could be 'switched out' for the mainlines only – where straight Absolute Block is in force – however due to the volume of traffic, and the daily use of the branch the 'box has never been fitted with a block switch. This possibility does not exist at the other 10 signalboxes on the patch, as all of them convert between different methods of working or supervise level crossings.

The Tunnel Jct – Droitwich Spa section has always been something of a bottleneck, especially since the abolition of Fernhill Heath 'box in 1970, which previously halved the section during busy periods, and switched out of circuit when not required. In 2008 the situation was eased by the installation of the first Intermediate Block section (IB) on the district. IBs were

introduced to abolish block posts that were needed purely to break up a lengthy section and didn't have another function, such as sidings. The signals are controlled by the 'box in rear and a track circuit between the original section signal and the IB signal form a new section. Depending on the length of the section a separate distant signal may be required for the IB, or sometimes it may be placed below the original section signal. As the signal is totally remote from the 'box a 'Train running away' alarm is fitted so that the signalman may act accordingly without delay should anything fail to stop. At Droitwich the up IB signals (home and distant) are roughly in the location of the old Fernhill Heath signals. On the down road no IB has been installed (which would need to be controlled from Tunnel Jct) but the old outer home signal (No.7) has been reinstated in rear of the platform. There was always a signal here, historically to protect the rear of trains standing in the platform, but as the train was still in the clearing point, and the tailamp could not be seen, the signalman could not send 'Train out of section' (2-1) and accept another train anyway, so the signal was removed as other safeguards, such as track circuit AB and Welwyn controls protect the train from the rear. The new No.7 signal is placed 200 yards from AB track circuit so a safety overlap is provided and a camera allows the signalman to observe the tail-lamp without the need of the train crew to use the telephone, or similar, to advise 'train

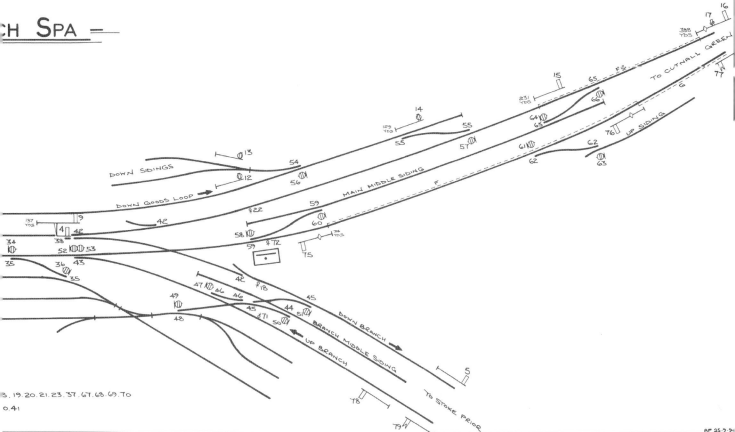

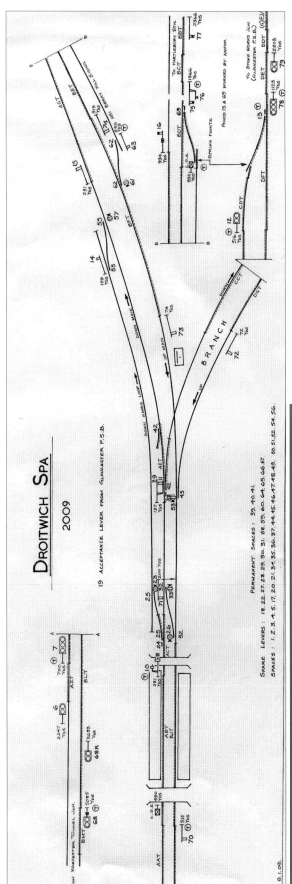

The rear of Droitwich 'box showing the GW nameplate (which has been stolen from the front) and the slightly unusual stairs due to the constricted space available at the ends. To the right of the entrance door is a very compact toilet cubicle. As a young apprentice the signalman here tried out his favourite 'wind up' on me. I obviously didn't react to a satisfactory level for him, so by way of punishment he waited for me to use the loo and shoved a flag pole in the door handle so I was trapped in there. After sufficient reaction - I am quite claustrophobic - I was released! The red and white chequered boards on the left corner indicate LIMITED CLEARANCE to trackside workers who could become trapped between the wall and a passing train. Although there is sufficient room to pass, there is not the minimum 4 feet which is required for a 'position of safety'.

The operating floor of Droitwich Spa with its levers spaced at 5¼". It is evident that some of the signalmen have not been using their lever cloths as the handles are not all shiny. Using the cloth doesn't just keep things polished, it is easier on the hands, and of course it is the signalman's badge of office. Historically the railway was always a family employer. Matthew Knight, the signalman seen here, is the third generation of his family to serve the railways around Worcester, working the same levers as his grandfather before him.

complete'. At the time of writing the camera has not proved very helpful at sighting the tail-lamps on multiple units, and so has not been relied upon. The fact that two redundant levers have been brought back into service is nice, especially as automatic signals worked by track circuits could have been an option throughout the section. The IB lever is painted red and yellow (as it works a stop and a distant signal together) and has a white stripe in the centre signifying that it is released from another 'box (in this case Tunnel Jct via LINE CLEAR on the block instrument) and so really is quite a colourful addition to any frame: see page 103.

The new outer home signal has made the signalman's job simpler as the junction points are no longer in the clearing point of 200 yards in advance of the home signal. Previously, having accepted a train from Tunnel Jct, the Down Main to Loop and Down Main to Down Branch points had to be maintained in their position until the approaching train was at a stand in the platform. It is easy to see that this could be something of a nuisance, if the train had not yet entered section and in the minute after accepting, one became in a position to reset the junction and pull off right through. A certain amount of discretion was used in the application of this rule in order to keep trains running smoothly, provided safety was not compromised. However the new signal (No.7) means that

the signalman may quite legitimately reverse the junction with a LINE CLEAR pegged up. As well as considering junctions within the 'clearing point' there is also 'flank protection' fitted to double junctions, such as those at Droitwich Spa. Before the Down Main to Branch points (No.42) may be reversed, the from Branch to Up Main points (No.43) must be pulled. This ensures anything inadvertently running back will be diverted from a conflicting move on the diamond crossing.

Working Droitwich Spa 'box is enough to keep anyone fit. The bell signals are pretty frequent throughout the day, and the lengthy lever frame requires plenty of pacing up and down. There is lots of 'pulling off' and lots of 'checking in' trains, signal to signal - often from all three sides at once. Although the 'box doesn't receive many visitors in human form, there was, in my time a very fluffy 'box cat which would ask to be let in and out between trains, adding to the hustle and bustle of the place. Once upon a time many 'boxes had a cat to keep the rodent population down, which was probably very wise. Despite regular visits from the rat man every 'box I worked at had something scurrying about downstairs, or sometimes even on the operating floor – regrettably I never got the chance to work at Droitwich so I'm unable to comment on the efficacy of the cat.

9

Henwick

Across the River Severn, in the St. John's area is Henwick 'box which is on the road of the same name. Henwick is perhaps the forgotten corner of the Worcester triangle, and is often overlooked, but does in fact have an important claim to fame as the oldest mechanical signalbox in Worcestershire. Residents of this part of the city cannot forget the 'box though for its busy level crossing is the cause of many a hold-up for local road users. Innocent bystanders may presume that the man inside the 'box merely raises and lowers the crossing barriers, but since the 1973 resignalling, he is now responsible for the junction between the Worcester and Hereford railway, and the Birmingham line, which as we have already seen is referred to as the 'Droitwich Loop' in the signalboxes. Henwick also assumes responsibility for Foregate Street Station and so the signalman is often busy with trains which don't actually pass the 'box, but terminate in the platform and return whence they came. When I first went to Henwick the S&T lineman for the district, Geoff Finch, remarked "this is about the only 'box you'll ever see that uses EVERY lever in the frame, EVERY day!" As the detonator levers – used only in emergency - were in a separate little frame beside the main levers this was a true enough statement.

Built in C.1875 Henwick was a McKenzie and Holland signalling contractors design, to GWR specification, although closer inspection will reveal obvious signs of an extension, reported to have been in 1897. The 25 lever frame dates from then, and again is interesting as it is, a now rare GW double twist interlocking. The actual mechanism downstairs has now been converted to the tappet system (as generally employed elsewhere on the WR) but on the operating floor the generous sweeps and the almost vertical appearance of the levers show that this is certainly a veteran piece of engineering. Henwick originally controlled the typical station layout found all along the route, although with the additional sidings for the power station, where coal was unloaded onto a conveyor belt, and later a full goods loop on the up side. Many signalboxes of this variety would only be open for the morning shift to shunt goods traffic, or to break up long sections as required, but due to the level crossing Henwick was open continuously. Nowadays there is no night traffic so the Malvern line may close between the last train at night and the first one in the morning (saving about 5 hours wages at four locations each day). As a night turn signalman at Worcester, the herald of the new day was 5-5-5 (Opening signalbox) chiming out from Henwick, followed by an acceptance light for testing purposes.

Opposite page - *The interior of Henwick 'box. The 'upright' appearance of the levers and the generous 'sweeps' between levers of the double twist frame are apparent in this view. The view was taken during what was a rare lull in traffic as both Acceptance Levers and the Block Instruments are at Normal. The WR signalbox diagrams are works of art in their own right, being hand drawn, with beautiful flowing curves and neat stencilled lettering, by the Reading drawing office. Beneath the signalbox diagram hangs a gradient profile chart for the Worcester and Hereford line. Before the days of continuous train brakes, it was vital that a signalman knew his gradients so that the likely course of any breakaway or runaway vehicles could be predicted. Nowadays a signalman should still know the gradients on his patch but should any couplings detach, the train should come to an immediate halt.*

Right - *Signalman Philip Elwell between trains at Henwick. Sadly, since the taking of this photograph the signalman's pipe – once such a part of the scene – has been outlawed.*

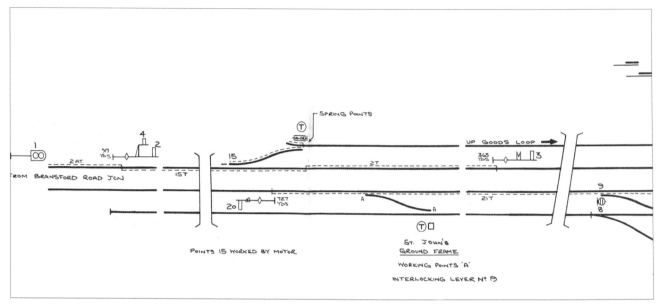

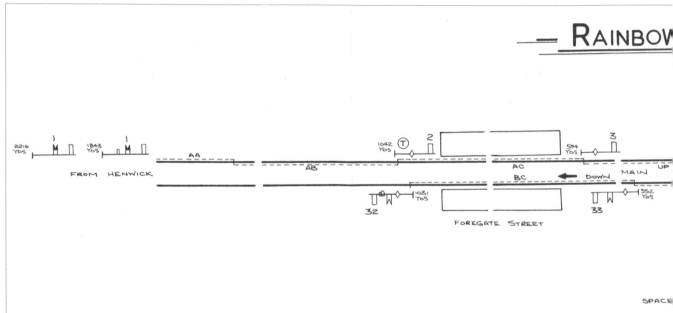

Rainbow Hill Junction signalbox formerly controlled the Western point of the triangle, and after the closure of Foregate Street 'box in '59, its area of control was extended slightly to cover the platforms in the station. This was effected by motorised semaphore signals, in the same place as those controlled by the former overhead 'box at the station. When Rainbow Hill was closed the junction was removed altogether and so the lines from Shrub Hill and Tunnel Jct run parallel, but independently, through Foregate Street station. Trains regain the 'correct' line at Henwick - where conventional double line running restarts - via the old trailing crossover, similar to Norton Jct. A new facing crossover provides access for up trains to either route. One quirk of the new layout is that platform 1, on the 'Branch' is in Henwick's station limits, thanks to the starting signal No.5, whereas platform 2 on

the Droitwich line is in the block section to Tunnel Jct. The signal at the end of platform 2 is Tunnel Jct's home signal (No.20), allowing terminating trains to shunt out and back from platform 2 using the 5-2/2-5 move described in the Tunnel Jct chapter. Up trains may enter platform 1 under Henwick's authority with no acceptance needed from Shrub Hill, which is useful when trains are following one another in the late evening to get back to shed. However, this caused some problems for trains which terminated at Foregate Street on the Branch. For years these trains had to continue over the level crossing, clearing the single line track circuit (FG) in order to normalise the acceptance lever at Henwick. The train could then be readmitted to the platform from disc signal No.11 and treated like an ordinary up train. Some of these services went into the siding at Henwick to await their

HENWICK

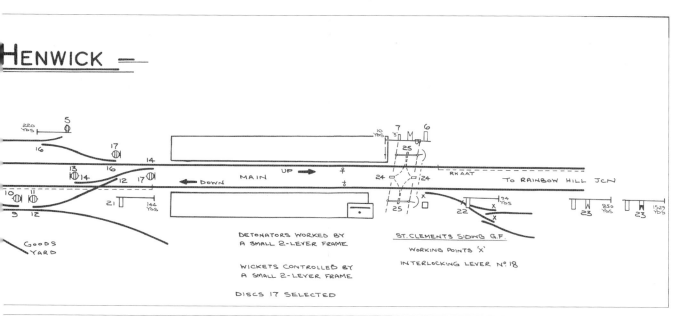

HILL JCN

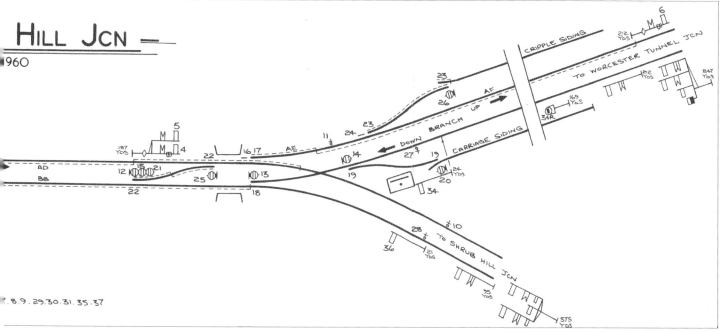

path, hence the "every lever used" claim. This shunt move officially involves the train drawing forward beyond No.11, then shunting back behind No.14 (which involves a 5-2 release from Tunnel Jct as the train is now 'in section' on the Droitwich Loop) and then entering the siding. Of course, all that takes some time, and as it is possible to set the points into the Up Refuge siding from the Down Branch, most trains would be 'talked by' the home signal (No.23) to go straight in. Facing moves from running lines into dead end sidings are rarely signalled in WR practice.

In 2006, the circuitry was altered so that trains may turn around in platform 1 without the need to traverse the viaduct and level crossing first, in order to save a precious few minutes for trains, and to prevent closing the road. Although proper signalmen are unworried about necessary delay to road traffic – after all it is the railway

that pays them, not the motorist – it is a lot less hassle for all concerned. As the modern railway terms the method of signalling as Track Circuit Block, it was deemed acceptable for the acceptance lever to be replaced with a stationary train on FG track circuit in order that it be offered back to Shrub Hill. Normalising the acceptance lever with a train in section totally contradicts the principle of the WR Acceptance Lever Block system, although as the terminating train is changing direction it now becomes out of the section - a complex, but important distinction. As the track circuits are protecting the train it is quite safe, there is also the added safeguard of a signalman at each end. Modern installations rely solely on the correct functioning of track circuits, which is considered sufficient. The older methods have a more 'belt and braces' approach and are therefore better in my

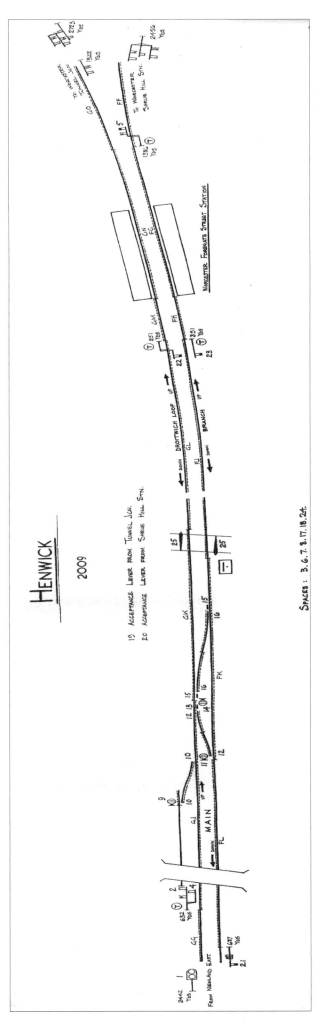

opinion. Once a terminating train has stopped in Foregate Street the acceptance lever may be replaced and the train offered back as normal. A bellcode is sent to Shrub Hill to advise that the train is at a stand, although this information is more important for the man at Henwick really. Rather than use the 3-3-4 (Train or vehicles at a stand) code already in the book, a special code of 3-1-3 is authorised. I wonder if those who thought it up realised they were reintroducing the old signal for a GW railcar?

To assist station and level crossing work there is a bell between the platform staff and signalmen and trains are 'belled' in and out of the platform using the following codes: 2 Branch (down), 4 Branch (up), 3 Droitwich Loop (down), 5 Droitwich Loop (up). When the 4 bells is received from the platform then the ordinary 'Train entering section' (2 bells) can be sent to Shrub Hill, if the train has been accepted. In the case of a train which is waiting acceptance in the platform, the description would be sent again at this point, to emphasise that the refused train is now actually standing and waiting for the off. The Shrub Hill signalman may often wait for this second reminder before accepting, so the junction is not locked up with a train that is not yet coming. In the down direction, the bell from the platform is the cue to lower the crossing barriers and pull off. There is also a treadle at both home signals (No.s 22 & 23) which sounds a buzzer in the 'box, so the signalman knows the train is actually waiting at the signal, and isn't still undertaking platform duties. This is especially useful if the train needs to be 'checked' for the down starter (No.21) because the platform may have belled the train out early, or forgotten. In GWR days there was a bell between the platform and the booking office and before dispatching a train the platform would ring the clerk, who could reply if his booking work was complete or request the foreman to wait for passengers still purchasing tickets. In these days of 'quality customer service experiences' the train will depart regardless of how many people are sprinting up the stairs.

The home signals are perched high on top of the viaduct, which runs from near the site of Rainbow Hill Jct, all the way across the city and over the river. No.23 was particularly exciting to climb up as the post is actually fixed to the viaduct's side and so the view down is a bit scary. There is an access platform at the base of the post, bracketed out from the wall, into which my maintenance gang were once crammed in order to be clear of the running line. Once the job had been done we set about returning to the platforms. There had obviously been some confusion as to what was going on because we thought there were no trains about, and the signalman thought we had finished. As we walked back a train approached from each direction. We all had to stand up on the viaduct wall and hold tight to the railings as the trains passed. I wasn't particularly perturbed by that, as it was all at low speed, but I was particularly annoyed that my cap was blown off onto a neighbouring rooftop. Of course, everybody else laughed. Nowadays maintenance staff are not allowed to go into such places when trains are moving.

Towards Newland East the line continues pretty much as it always has, and is signalled by normal Absolute Block.

Newland provides routing information by the suffix 3-4 for trains taking the Droitwich Loop. During my time on the patch this was added to the 'Train entering section' signal, the 2-3-4 being a satisfying little rhythm to tap out on the bell – rather akin to the football chant. Later this was amended to going on the end of the 'Is Line Clear…?' description in order to "standardise the bell codes." Despite several enquiries I've been unable to ascertain exactly why the routing code was sent differently here, other than the fact that "it's always been done that way" although I'm sure a reason once presented itself. Sadly, with efforts to standardise everything, little peculiarities such as this will be lost forever. It's curious that standardisation of bell codes is seen as worthwhile, when everything else at Worcester is condemned as non-standard by modern perspectives.

The crossing is closed for Up Droitwich trains immediately 'Train entering section' is received from Newland or when the berth track circuit (GG) is occupied for trains bound for the Branch, as the distant signal (No.1) cannot be cleared for this route. The down distants are fixed at caution as the speed restriction over the crossovers is severe.

Relief men usually moaned about having to go to Henwick, the crossovers being regarded as the heaviest of pulls on the district, and the impatience of motorists being cited as a reason to avoid the place. However the resident men at Henwick seem to like the place, it being a busy little spot, with a good grade and no night shift. In 2007 it won the resurrected 'best kept signalbox' competition on the region, proving the pride taken in the place by the regulars. During 2003 I visited Henwick on a few afternoons having finished a morning shift at my own 'box. It was a splendid place to sit by the window with a cup of tea to watch the world go by. I had once been told that an irate motorist threw a bag of something unmentionable through the open window, in retaliation for having the barriers closed in front of him, but I only found the place pleasing, with pedestrians smiling in acknowledgment as they passed by, and the occasional toot of a taxi driver being the only disturbance. On one afternoon I was there the signalman pressed the LOWER button, to start the red lights flashing sequence. As the yodels sounded a gang of school kids walking home broke into a sprint to get across before the gates swung down. Although there is a pedestrian underpass this seemed the norm for lads of a certain age. On this day, as the entrance gates began to come down, all the boys ducked under it and ran to freedom. All except the last boy, who was rather rotund, wheezing and struggling to catch up, but by no means slowing down. The signalman guffawed loudly "Oh this little chap often plays this game with me" and still the boy charged on. The gates slammed shut against the road and the boy, now going far too fast to pull up in time collided beautifully with the barrier, recoiling onto his bottom. The boy raised his fist at the signalbox and shouted something suitably insulting at the signalman,

whilst catching his breath. "Ah…." said the signalman turning on his heel to clear the signals "splendid little fellow that one…plenty of vim!" seemingly oblivious to the obscenities that were being directed at him across the street. Although there would have been less road traffic, the days when this box had traditional gates, worked by wheel from the signalbox must have been interesting.

There was a large empty yard at Henwick, where the station and sidings had once been. There was rumour that one day the station could reopen, providing commuters from this side of the river with somewhere to park their cars and catch the train. There was also a suggestion that a power signalling installation at Worcester would be best sited here, and able to monitor its level crossing from the windows. Despite these ideas, the railway has since sold all the land off and a medical centre occupies the site now. Henwick signalbox is all that remains of the old railway in this end of the city. Perhaps someone in an office somewhere took pity on this old place when deciding its fate almost 40 years ago. All the technology was available to control everything electrically, or even remotely, but the ancient lever frame and semaphores signals (few of which are near the signalbox and require motors) were all retained. Henwick is an important reminder of why the Worcester patch is special in the 21st century. I am fortunate in having a piece of this history in the form of an old arm from the down starter (No.21) which was quite battered by shots taken at it by the local thuggery, and so was replaced. In an amazing coincidence the serial number printed on the top edge of the arm is my initials followed by the year of my birth – the arm is now part of the signal which stands proudly at my garden gate!

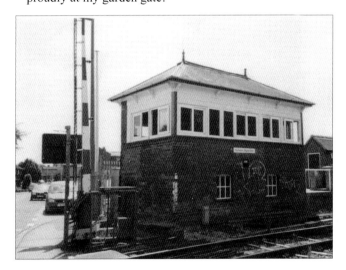

Henwick Signalbox as seen from the level crossing. The alterations to this old 'box are less obvious from the front view, although from the rear clear signs of an extension can be seen. There is a small window in the rear wall to allow the signalman to spot approaching vehicles.

10

Newland East

Originally opened as 'Stocks Lane Crossing Signal Box' in 1900, Newland East is another GW type 7(a) - probably the archetypal Great Western signalbox. On completion, the new signalbox was responsible for the adjacent level crossing and little else, besides a crossover and refuge siding, which almost every 'box had once upon a time. Between 18th March 1929 and 5th April 1965 there was a halt at Newland, with the up platform staggered on the Worcester side of the road and the down platform opposite the signalbox. The 'box was renamed to match the adjacent station (and to avoid confusion with the other Stocks Lane crossing on the GW mainline). Apart from the brief passage of trains the job must have been a peaceful, sleepy one, with little hustle and bustle.

In 1943 the signalbox took on a new role, for sidings and a loop line was laid between the halt and the gasworks signalbox, not far outside Malvern Link. The new 'Newland' complex was used for military purposes, and the controlling signalboxes were appropriately re-christened Newland East and Newland West. A second hand frame of 33 levers, the date of which is unknown was fitted in Newland East. Although I don't know what was there before it is unlikely the original layout required as many levers. The new frame is a GW 3 bar VT, which now utilises 5 bar VT locking. At some point, perhaps when the larger frame was installed, a small extension was added to the end of the 'box for the broom cupboard etc. Conveniently this has recently been converted into the signalman's toilet facilities, and the dreadful Portaloo is no more. Between 1954 and 1964 the depot was used for the pre assembly of track panels, and had its own shunting engine fussing about, in between deliveries and despatches from the mainline.

Strangely, things at Newland have rather gone full circle. Apart from the removal of the box's splendid chimney, it is now much as it was in 1900. There is no depot, no station halt, no West 'box, and except the occasional train shooting past, total tranquillity. The Down Refuge siding was retained initially but as its use would be limited to emergencies only it was lifted by the 1990s. The crossover however is still available for use, and really could prove very useful indeed. There was talk in the late '90s of its removal, to save on maintenance costs, but the local inspector fought for it to remain quite sensibly, and it did. There are two quite busy stations between Newland and Malvern Wells and if anything were to happen at one of them, it is a long way back to Worcester for a waiting or assisting train – that's when the crossover at Newland East could become invaluable. Despite the neighbouring signalboxes being less than 5 miles away on each side, Newland is a very important link in the chain, as a blockpost, for its splits up a busy section. Although the Malvern section is not vast in mileage, every train calls at Malvern Link and Great Malvern, and many trains take time to reverse at Malvern Wells, meaning that traffic often queues at Newland. If it had been converted to an automatic crossing and the signals removed then today's timetable simply couldn't work. It is frequently the case that there are four trains in Newland's area of control at one time, two coming towards, and two going away. It is not totally implausible that two others may be waiting there as well.

Opposite - Looking South West from Newland past the crossover which was retained by fierce protest, and across to the striking Malvern Hills.
Right - Newland East Signalbox. The well proportioned GW design is the height of simplicity, yet elegance, I think. The porch is a later extension. The relays which work the electrical interlocking are housed in the silver lineside cabinets next to the road, as there is not enough equipment here to justify a separate relay room. This signalbox once had a substantial chimney. Similarly designed 'boxes built after this date were given stovepipes instead, as 'pot-bellied' stoves were more efficient at heating draughty signalboxes than open fires. Unfortunately all the Worcester signalboxes have lost their real fires now, and the welcoming atmosphere that they instantly provided.

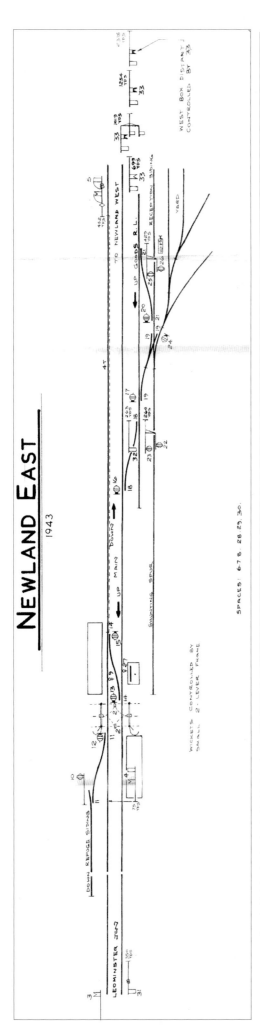

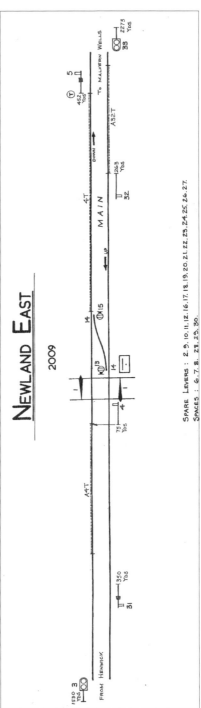

Newland East was once described to me as 'the 'box from the book'. In other words, it is the only signalbox on the district that works plain Absolute Block in both directions, with a distant, home and starter signal on both roads. It is exactly the sort of layout that is used in the book of regulations to explain the method of signalling, with the addition of a level crossing of course. Towards the end of 2003 when I was well settled in at Shrub Hill I asked the inspector, Mr. Gardner if I could go and learn another 'box. I had been fortunate in keeping the Cotswold line 'boxes 'in ticket' but there was not much call to go to any of them because an influx of new staff had meant there were no gaps on the roster. He was understandably wary of letting me take overtime to go and learn other places, when I was officially a resident man elsewhere, but there were to be some vacancies on the route and it was thought advantageous to have some chaps to fill in now and again. However, there simply wasn't the time for me to go and learn somewhere complex like Droitwich, so I opted for Newland East, and he agreed if I could pass out quickly.

I went for a few hours one afternoon to have a look at the place. There was no service to learn as trains simply went up or down, and there were no real intricacies to remember about the place. The routing code business was a simple case - if it was a headcode I knew, the train was going through Shrub Hill, and if it was one I didn't know, it must be for the Droitwich Loop and therefore need the 2-3-4 sent for it. There is an annunciator in Malvern Link station, which is the reminder to lower the barriers for up trains. Non-stopping up trains need the barriers lowered immediately the train is put 'on line' from Malvern Wells, but that is only empty stock or special trains. Down trains had no annunciator and most of the men put the gates down after a minute or two had passed from the time 'Train entering section' (2 bells) was received from Henwick. I was advised that an egg timer was a good idea in case the phone or whatever else distracted you – since then an official timer has been added to the block shelf. I remembered years before, visiting the place and pulling off for a train in each direction and then Dave Pagett saying "and now stand well back!" This was the only 'box I ever worked where two trains could pass at speed, and I thought he was referring to the accompanying 'whoosh' and rattle of the windows as the trains rushed by,

Inside Newland East 'box. The simple layout means the block shelf is not cluttered much beyond the essential block instruments and bells. All four indicators point to TRAIN ON LINE demonstrating the steady flow of traffic past the box. This box now has two more white (spare) levers since the abolition of the detonator placers. When operated these put two 'shots' - creating an extra loud 'bang', on either the Up or Down lines. Now any signalman needing to use detonators in an emergency situation will take longer to do so, as they must be placed by hand.

but then he said "it's a bit too easy here to put back in front of one if you're not careful…." He was right actually. Newland East is the only signalbox on the patch which doesn't have an illuminated diagram. The track circuits are repeated in little indicators on the block shelf (CLEAR or OCCUPIED). It was only when layouts started to become very complex that indications in the diagram became common place. Anyway, I found myself constantly looking at the diagram to check the train had passed the starting signals – and of course there was never anything lit up! I had to retrain myself to look out of the window instead, which took some getting used to, but fortunately I managed not to replace anything in error. The starting signals (Nos. 5 & 31) are back-locked to the level crossing interlocking lever, so the barriers cannot be raised until these signals are replaced. This is an example of conditional locking, as the starting signals can be pulled with the barriers up (lever 1 reverse) or with the barriers

down (lever 1 normal) but the barrier lever cannot be altered once the signals are cleared. The best practise to get into was to do all the bells and train register times first, and then start putting the levers back carefully. Being in too much of a hurry to open the crossing and waiting, hands poised on levers, for trains to pass is bound to go wrong one day. Not much else happened that day but it was pleasant to chat with Anna, Worcester's only lady signalman. She had been the voice of Worcester's railway for me, for several years before, when she did the train announcements at Foregate Street station in her inimitable style. I don't recall much else about the afternoon, as I don't expect much railway training went on, but I know I was very impressed with the view of the Malvern Hills and the quaint little farm opposite, with its ducks and hens scratching about completed the atmosphere. Rural Worcestershire at its best.

The barrier controls are mounted on a pedestal in the same corner where the mechanical gate wheel once stood. The flags on the window sill remain an essential part of the signal box equipment.

The next day Paul Gardner came to ask a few questions and Newland East was added to the list of signalboxes for which I was 'passed as competent'. I doubted that I would get a turn there for a while but fortunately a Friday morning shift was free at the end of my usual stint of earlies.

I set off in good time for my 5.15 start and everything got into full swing quite quickly. Unlike the Cotswolds line, where one could relax into the shift gently, the Malvern line is 'all systems go' straight away. Despite seeming a simple job, I took a while to settle in, with the continuous feeling that I must be forgetting something – perhaps it was too straightforward? As everything was running to time, there were no hold ups of any sort and I thought to myself that if it weren't for the barriers I could probably 'switch out' and go home! I had, by now got into the hang of looking out of the window, and not at the diagram, and felt at home in the place, other than the fact that the train register was on the 'wrong' side, compared with what I was used to. Then the barriers failed to rise after the passage of a train. Annoyingly the barrier lever was also stuck reversed – if it had stuck normal then the signalling of trains would have been quite unaffected, but as such my home signals were locked. It is possible for a signalman to manually raise the barriers during such a fault, but as the rail traffic was so regular there really wouldn't be much of a margin to do so between trains. As there is a reasonable diversion for cars, I decided to leave the gates, tell motorists that the equipment had failed and deal with the trains, whilst waiting for the S&T. Unfortunately during my very brief training day I had not

been told that ROAD CLOSED signs were hiding beneath the 'box for such an eventuality, so I went out and spoke to the drivers every 5 minutes or so. One such motorist was not at all impressed, but I was not sufficiently moved to start delaying trains to let him across.

When the home signal cannot be cleared for some reason it is sometimes permissible to use a yellow flag to indicate to the driver that he may pass the signal at danger and draw up to the signalbox. As there are no facing points at Newland this is one location where such a rule comes in handy, especially as telephones are not fitted to all the signals. So when each train approached I would clear the starting signal and exhibit my yellow flag when the train was almost at a stand. The driver would give a long toot on the horn and proceed slowly up to the 'box, where he could be advised of the circumstances and told to continue obeying signals as normal. A green flag is shown at the end of the message as authority to proceed. I went through this procedure several times, three times with the same driver who was now on his second trip to Malvern and back. On his return (which would have been his fourth receipt of the message "There is a barrier failure, proceed with caution over the crossing and obey all other signals") I held out the yellow flag in good time for his approach to the home signal (No.32). He gave a long blast and proceeded past the home signal at a reasonable pace, seeing that the starting signal was off and that my yellow had rapidly changed to a green, accompanied by a 'keep going' hand gesture from me. By the time he reached the 'box he had built up a decent pace and gave a friendly toot and wave whilst flying through. The sound of the train masked the sounds of feet on the steps. It was the inspector and his assistant who burst through the door with "What on earth's going on here?!" "It's OK. Everything's under control" I replied. He looked non-plussed but asked no more questions. I suppose it wasn't quite to the letter of the law, but I didn't think there much point in bringing him to a stand again, when there really was no message to give at all that the flags hadn't already given. I did feel rather Victorian that day, doing half of my signalling via flags out of the window!

Mr. Gardner had a chat about various things and then Geoff Finch of the S&T arrived and put the fault in order – it was something to do with a power supply. He stopped for a little chat, but as his shift time was running out he made for home shortly afterwards. Then I had a little chat on the box to box phone, for my regular mate at Tunnel Jct happened to be 'guesting' at Malvern Wells that day, as coincidence would have it. Les finished the call "splendid – all the best then". I had never known him to say anything else at the end of any conversation. Little did we know that that first eventful day at Newland East would be my last at that 'box, and indeed, my last day (officially) working any signalbox for the Western Region.

11

Malvern Wells

Malvern Wells signalbox is the last survivor of a handful of 'boxes bearing the name 'Malvern' between Newland and Colwall tunnel. In Great Western appendices the 'box is referred to as 'Malvern Wells Station' and its close neighbour 'Malvern Wells Tunnel' although the actual nameplate had no suffix, according to other sources. This signalbox has a rather interesting history and although its functions have certainly evolved through its existence, it retains a very unspoilt feel. The 'box originally would have been installed to control the usual station facilities, as we have seen all along the line, and would have been switched into circuit as traffic requirements demanded. One imagines Malvern Wells to have been a peaceful station, unlike its 'Great' and 'Link' counterparts. The tunnel signalbox would have been open continuously, because the tunnel to Colwall is of single bore only. The other bore, that can still be seen today, is an older tunnel that fell into disuse on being replaced, so trains have always been forced to navigate a single line section here. However, unlike other wayside stations there was also the descriptively named 'Malvern and Tewkesbury Junction' 'box a few chains up the line, with its own coal sidings and small engine shed. This made Malvern Wells a centre of activity as goods loops between the tunnel and the station, and from the junction towards the Wells were laid. It was also a convenient site for the WR engine shed, as space at Great Malvern was limited. I don't know if the natural water supply was chemically 'good' for steam engines, but it certainly is good to drink, and even today the signalbox has its own supply on tap from the famous spring.

In 1954 the junction signalbox to the LMR line was closed and the Down Goods Loop was put under the control of Malvern Wells signalbox. At the same time an early piece of rationalisation was undertaken by the WR. The single line points near the tunnel were motorised, enabling Malvern Wells to take control, making the tunnel signalbox obsolete. During the 50s there were a few examples of this 'centralising', the idea being that if the tunnel 'box had to be manned all the time, and didn't do a great deal of lever work, combining the two made economic sense. The Up Goods Loop was truncated into a refuge siding – there had been private siding facilities at the 'old tunnel' end previously. In 1965, the other Malvern stations lost their signalboxes, as they did their goods facilities, and simply became platforms aside the double line. Malvern Wells however, had coal traffic and the vital single line control and so the signalbox outlived the station after which it was named. Any trains terminating at Malvern must now go through to 'the Wells' before returning to Worcester, which is a simple matter in these days of multiple unit trains. Great Malvern station, despite

having lost its signalling, and its imposing clock tower, is still rather grand by today's standards. There is still a private covered entrance to the girl's college (though disused) and the ornate metalwork of the platform canopy is colourfully decorated. Although, once upon a time, it really would have been quite a place. The GWR appendix from 1943 states that the use of engine whistles must be kept to an absolute minimum in the vicinity of Great Malvern, whose residents must have been rather exclusive to warrant such consideration – and with a war on!

In 1967 further rationalisation of the route saw the whole Ledbury-Malvern section singled and so Colwall and Ledbury North End signalboxes, which had hung on a little longer than others, became redundant in the October. So Malvern Wells, a GW type 7d of 1919, with its 3 bar VT frame of 40 levers, is all that is left of this former hub of the railways in West Malvern. However, as all these alterations were carried out in the 1960s, the signalling that remains has a very traditional feel to it. There are not many track circuits, few clever

Single line Lock & Block instrument and double line Absolute Block instrument side by side at Malvern Wells.

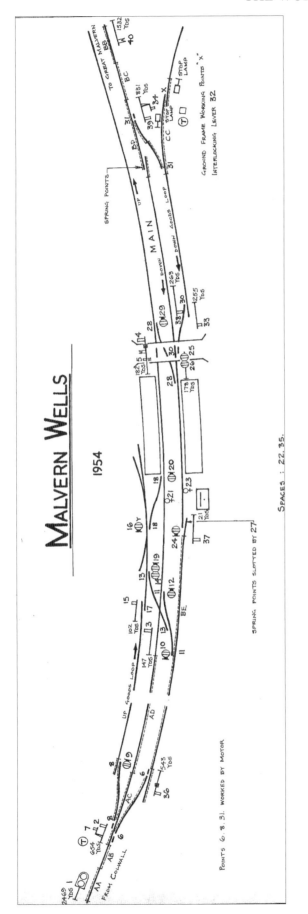

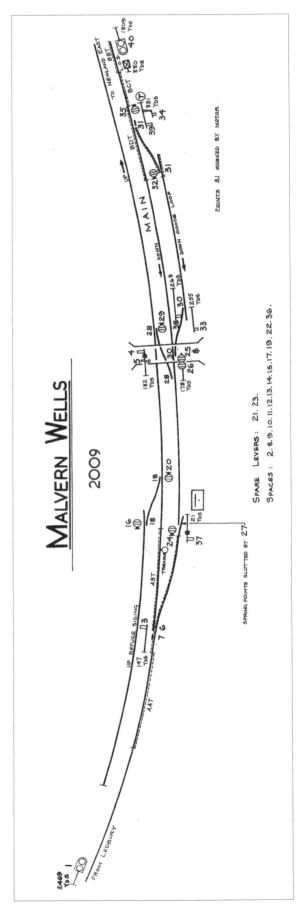

timers or electrical safeguards, and the signalman, with nothing more high tech than a lever collar, or a glance out of the window, presides over all to ensure the safety of trains. This is particularly noticeable at the Worcester end of the layout, where visibility is quite restricted under the bridge, and where trains frequently stand to turn back and form a new service. There are no track circuits at this point and all wise signalmen immediately collar the down inner home signal (No.38) on replacing it, to prevent another train being inadvertently signalled into the rear of the terminating train. Although one imagines that a signalman couldn't possibly forget that which is going on immediately in front of his nose, it is sometimes the most obvious thing that gets overlooked. The worst railway disaster ever, at Quintinshill in 1915, was the result of a signalman forgetting a train standing outside his 'box.

It was often said that the Wells was a much better place to work than Newland, as you only saw each train once! It is indeed the case that much of the days work is taken up with terminating trains crossing over and returning, but there is also the added interest of 'looping' trains to allow another to pass, and in the morning empty stocks used to run coupled into the Down Goods Loop, and then split to form two departures from Great Malvern. As well as the superb scenery, it is certainly the most popular signalbox on the line from an operating point of view.

As the line through the tunnels has always been single track, a system was installed which allowed these short, yet mainline, sections to be run without the need for a physical token. The 'Lock and Block' system is essentially like an Absolute Block instrument for a single line. There is an up and down indicator with the same three positions as the double line equivalent. However, the commutator of the Lock and Block is electrically locked in position by the sequence of events outside. When a train is accepted (in the normal way using standard bellcodes) the commutator is turned clockwise to show LINE CLEAR, which is repeated at the 'box in rear. The commutator cannot then be restored to the normal position until it has been turned clockwise again to TRAIN ON LINE, and the train has actually passed through the section. This is proved by an exit treadle at each end of the section, and as the train passes over it a TREADLE CLEARED indication pops up in a little aperture above the handle. Only then can the instrument be normalised. As with all the systems we have seen though, there has to be a 'loophole' for trains that need to be cancelled off after they have been accepted. This is achieved by means of a 'send release' or 'receive release' lever on both instruments. On sending the cancelling signal (3-5) the release lever can be swung, causing the treadle indication to appear and allowing the instrument to be returned to normal. When everything is restored the 3-5 bell signal is acknowledged. There is a mechanical counter on the release levers on both instruments which logs the number of releases sent/ received. The signalmen at each end write this number in the register every time a cancellation is made. This system

doesn't totally prevent human error, but it does mean that every release requires the co-operation of both men and is recorded. Since the reintroduction of HSTs on Malvern services this procedure is widely used to turn round sets on the single line at the Wells. When the section was singled throughout this clever system was simply extended in length. It begs the question that if such a simple system was available all those years ago, why was antiquated token working put into use on the Cotswolds line when it was singled? However WR Lock and Block working was never widespread, and the remaining instruments at Malvern Wells and Ledbury are the only two working examples which, I'm told, are bound for the National collection one day. Under the GW the system was governed by the ETT regulations, as far as they could apply in the absence of a token. Today, they are covered by Tokenless Block regulations, with modified signalbox instructions. The strange thing about Tokenless Block regulations is that they were designed much later on and mainly for use on lightly trafficked rural routes, particularly on the Scottish Region. Failures with the signalling on such routes could result in huge delays and so dispensation is given to work with paper tickets in the event of a block failure until a Pilotman is available. No such relaxation of standards is allowed with ETT working, the regulations of which have probably not changed much since its invention. So now we have another example of perverse double standards, which the piecemeal alteration of signalling has produced: the once double tracked mainline through the Cotswolds has trains stopping to pick up and set down tokens, and if anything goes wrong the trains must stop until a Pilotman is summoned. On the other hand, the single line section through the narrow tunnels of Malvern and Ledbury, which the GW went to special lengths to signal safely and efficiently, can be worked by paper ticket and all the systems totally bypassed in a failure scenario. I'm sure the ticket working is acceptably safe in theory; it just seems strange how the rules vary with circumstance.

I visited Malvern Wells many times when a friend of mine worked there; he had been a visitor to Evesham 'box years before, until one day he decided to make his signalling professional. In those days you could get on the train at Worcester and a friendly driver would drop you off at the 'box whilst changing ends. I suppose I only have a very narrow minded view of the place as I only saw it on pleasant evenings when everything was running reasonably to time. At the end of the visit a red flag would be displayed to a terminating train to indicate that the driver should pull up to the 'box for a message to be given. The message was of course "hello mate, can I have a lift back to Evesham?"

Anyone who ever studied GW layouts will notice that signalboxes are very often in a dangerous place should anything run off the trap points – this was certainly the case at Malvern Wells. During a recent engineers possession, the signalman went home leaving the trap

The interior of Malvern Wells 'box, which is very homely indeed. At the left hand end of the shelf is a very shiny copper bell . This is the 'tell tale' alarm to warn of an occurrence within the confines of the tunnel.
The charming display of house plants and book shelves add to the cosy atmosphere and gives the signalmen something with which to pass the time. Most signalmen have a hobby of some sort, which they can take to work. I have known guitar practice, photography, watercolour painting, model making, parrot training and gardening to name a few.

Malvern Wells Signalbox. The contrast between the red and blue engineering brick work is particularly distinct, and pleasing here, unlike the opposing ventilator caps on the roof. To the right is the new air-conditioned relay room which has greatly relieved the cramped conditions in the locking room of the signalbox. To the left is the 'posh portaloo'. The resident signalman was intrigued by PTS* cat, who only ever crossed the line by entering through the official gate and then along the authorised walking route provided for railway staff.
* PTS - is the obligatory Personal Trackside Safety Certification for railway staff.

points (No.27) in the normal position, that is open, to throw off anything which rolls back from the tunnel. A breakdown in communications must have occurred because the tamping machine driver thought he had the route set to come through and passed the home signal at danger, went up the down line and derailed in front of the 'box. Had it been a train going at usual speed I doubt much of the 'box would have been left standing…..There was a requirement at the 'box to maintain the facing points (No.6) at normal whilst a down train was in section, so that anything accidentally rolling back would be put off at

the traps, only before accepting an up train from Ledbury, can the points be reversed and FPL No.7 locked – necessary for the 200 yards clearing point. Anyway, since the derailment the trap points have been removed altogether and I doubt will be replaced as they are increasingly disappearing from the modern railway. On my last visit I noticed a label on the loop exit points (No.30A) saying 'trailing moves only' as the points were not closing correctly. Hopefully then any runaway would be conveniently derailed here, which is far preferable to demolishing the nice signalbox.

12

Ledbury

The final location, at the western tip of the district, is Ledbury in the county of Herefordshire. Although nowadays it really appears as something of an 'out-station' its signalling history is rather more interesting. 'Ledbury Signalbox' – the only one remaining today – was once the middle of three, although it never had an official suffix to its name on the front. As at Malvern, there was a signalbox at the north end of the tunnel, to control the single line connection which was entitled 'Ledbury North End' from 1937, when a new 'box was constructed there. The date of the earlier signalbox 'Ledbury Tunnel Jct' is uncertain, although its nameplate was ordered in 1900 along with Ledbury's, so was probably contemporaneous with the original station signalbox, which was in use by 1881. The reason for the name change is also unclear, but the newer name was more descriptive of the 'box's function I feel. Although there was pointwork for the single line it was not a junction in the pure sense.

At the station end there was a proper junction, with the branch to Gloucester curving away to the south. The station itself was entitled 'Ledbury Junction' until 1959 when the route via 'Ledbury Town Halt' was closed. Originally the branch was double track to Dymock, but in 1917 this was reduced to a single line. In order to work the single line connections, a small signalbox 'Ledbury Branch' with just 6 levers was installed, so that the actual double junction could be retained and worked as before from Ledbury 'box. It was a short lived affair, for in 1925 power operated points meant the whole lot could be controlled from the main 'box and it was abolished, extending the token section from Dymock to Ledbury Junction Station. Therefore, Ledbury signalbox was quite a hive of activity in quite a small 'box. The building, of 1885, is a McKenzie and Holland (signalling contactors) type 3 design with pleasing arched brickwork and striking finial spikes. It is the only 'box in the area to have a flat wooden ceiling inside, which certainly looks original, and a balcony at the north end, overlooking the tunnel mouth and the site of the former goods facility.

The signalbox obviously lost some of its equipment on closure of the branch, but closure of the North End 'box simply meant extending the Lock and Block section, as we saw at Malvern Wells. By the 80s the down home signal (No.40) had been converted to colour light operation, which was a valuable aid to drivers emerging from the very narrow bore tunnel. In steam days, mechanical clappers were fitted at the end of the tunnel so drivers knew they were nearing daylight and could be poised ready to peer through the billowing smoke. The rest of the alterations at Ledbury date from 1984 – a very late rationalisation scheme for the Worcester patch. The double line from Shelwick Junction (where the Worcester and Hereford meets the North and West route) was singled, with the 'box at Shelwick being abolished and control passing to Hereford (Ayleston Hill) via a mini panel. It was also the end for Stoke Edith signalbox, which was basically the same as Newland East in layout in its latter years. It is a shame that this reduction in line capacity was executed so late in the day. One imagines that if BR had waited just a few more years the job would never have been done? Absolute Block working was replaced with WR Tokenless Block on the new single section of nearly 12 miles, and Stoke Edith crossing was replaced with automatic half barriers, supervised from Ledbury. All signals at the south end of Ledbury station are colour lights and the whole loop is track circuited. The Up siding was removed at a later date, which accounts for the two starting signals (No.s 4 & 5) – one of which is quite superfluous. It is interesting to note that there is still a hole in the new footbridge to allow the signalman to check the down starting signal (No.39) as there always was in semaphore days.

WR Tokenless Block was devised for lightly trafficked single line routes, such as the ex-LSWR Salisbury to Exeter line, which the region inherited from the Southern region for a time. However, quite unlike the Scottish version which utilises block bells and traditional signalling methods, this system was intended for locations where the signalman was based on the station and had other duties, such as the booking office, to attend to. So there are no bells to answer, and no 'offering' or 'accepting' of trains in the historic way. The Tokenless Block instrument has a switch which may be placed at ACCEPT or NORMAL and two push buttons OFFER and TRAIN ARRIVED. There is also an indicator needle which looks a little like an Absolute Block indicator. According to the timetable the signalman in advance will turn his switch to ACCEPT, if he is in a position to do so, he may then carry on with his duties accordingly. The signalman in rear, when he wishes to send the train on, will press the OFFER button, causing the indicator needle to swing to the TRAIN ACCEPTED position, this is his permission to send the train forward and also the electrical release for the starting signal. When the train enters section it automatically rings a bell in the advance 'box (in place of the 'Train entering' bell code, 2 beats) and the needle swings automatically to TRAIN IN SECTION. When the train arrives at the next block post the signalman there may restore his switch to NORMAL and press TRAIN ARRIVED which restores the instrument to the NORMAL position, provided the circuitry agrees and everything has taken place in sequence. It is the sequential

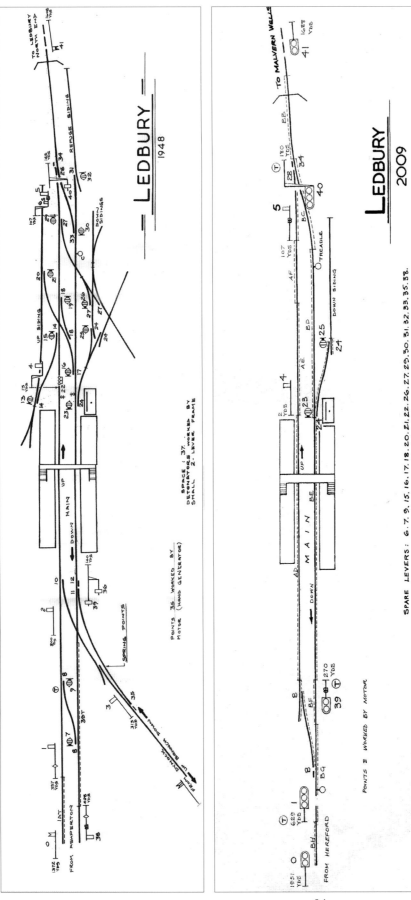

occupation and clearing of track circuits at each end which determines whether the section is clear or occupied. In case of emergency the signalman can replace his acceptance switch, which replaces the rear 'box's section signal to danger. If the power (or anything else for that matter) fails, the system's 'fail-safe' position is TRAIN IN SECTION.

The actual signalling in the passing loop is pretty much the same as other single line systems, although the interlocking allows both home signals to be pulled at the same time. The colour light home signals then bring the trains into the loop with a yellow aspect, under the approach control method. This obviously relieves the signalman of checking the approaching trains, leaving time to sell last minute tickets.

When the train arrives in the loop there is still the need to ensure the train is in complete with tailamp, before restoring the block and sending the next train into the section. At Ledbury this can be done visually for down trains. Train crews coming from Hereford must furnish the signalman with this information, as do at Evesham and similar places. In order to do this, a handy plunger is fitted on the up platform, which when depressed rings a little bell in the 'box and shows an indication 'Train arrived complete' assuring the signalman that it is safe to press the TRAIN ARRIVED button on the block instrument. This piece of equipment seems very useful to me, and far more efficient than waiting for a 'phone call as is the norm. Again, in the signalman/ booking clerk scenario for which this system was intended, this indication would be invaluable, removing the need for the man to be vigilant for hand signals etc. and remaining visible until such a time as it was necessary. A telephone call with such information might be confused if one was busy dealing with a queue of booking enquiries simultaneously. Of course, at Ledbury none of this

Ledbury Signalbox. The tall building at Ledbury looks impressive with its large lower windows and decorative finials. Most locking rooms are dark and dingy, but at Ledbury the downstairs is light and airy. The wooden staircase is a replacement, as modern regulations require a landing at the top of such steps. This one is reasonably in keeping with the old 'box fortunately, unlike the monstrous metal structures that the LMR have insisted in using on their mechanical 'boxes. The Ledbury signalman is not the only human presence on the station. There is a privately run booking office in a hut on the platform which is open in the mornings for ticket sales and information which must surely encourage more people to patronise the train service. Of course, on other lines where Tokenless Block was fitted it was intended the signalman would perform these duties too.

applies and an 'alright' wave from the guard would be quite sufficient, but nevertheless the equipment has been installed as per specification. Plungers for the same purpose are provided at Shelwick Junction and Hereford to advise Hereford Signalbox that the train has left the single line complete. The rather unexpected twist though, is that multiple unit passenger trains are exempt from the regulations and may be assumed as 'complete' on leaving the section at Shelwick. Quite why they may not be assumed complete at any other location on the WR employing similar systems, is a question nobody was ever able to answer. Obviously it can be appreciated that stopping a train especially for the guard to climb down and press the button at Shelwick is not desirable. As it is nearly always the same train which turns at Hereford to form the next up service, it is safe enough I suppose. It is strange though, and certainly flies in the face of all signalling principles.

Any out of course running or messages between signalboxes are conveyed by telephone. The local custom if the man at the other end has not accepted a train, is to give a buzz on the 'phone. Towards Malvern the trusty Lock and Block is operated conventionally and the signalman gets to act as a proper signalman complete with single stroke bells and full train register booking.

The narrow tunnel at Ledbury (and also at Malvern) has running through it a 'tell-tale' wire. Should a train fail in the tunnel or be stopped, the driver can sever the cable which causes a bell to sound in the controlling signalbox – thus summoning assistance. Only trains with a sliding or inward opening door for the driver and guard may pass through these tunnels with passengers aboard. A driver friend of mine once told me that even with the sliding door of a class 166 Turbo unit, it is still rather tight squeezing out of the cab for the more rotund gentlemen! The instructions for the operation of this tell-tale warn that the driver must coil the ends of the severed wire in such a manner that they cannot touch the wet walls of the tunnel, which may inadvertently conduct and cancel the warning bell.

In GW days, down trains were ordered to come to a stand before entering the tunnel to ensure that they made a controlled descent of the gradient – there was a sand drag at the North End into which runaways could be diverted. Today the trains are permitted to go straight into the hole, although there is still a set of trap points at the end of the Up (Main) loop, to prevent anything rolling back towards Hereford. The 'normal' position of these points is for the down loop, with the traps open, rather than the more usual arrangement where 'normal' is set for approaching trains, into the correct side of the passing loop. Once during my apprenticeship there was a curious fault at these set of points, which emphasised the vital importance of properly testing S&T equipment by the book. We had replaced the sets of microswitches on the motor points (No. 8 A&B) as the originals were due for renewal. One of our gang was up in the 'box to work the lever, as directed by a man on the ground with a mobile telephone. During the operation the point motors were isolated to protect our fingers and we manually pumped the points back and forth as was necessary. On completion of the work the request was given to put the lever to reverse. The points motored over and "reverse" was hollered down the 'phone, as confirmation that the indicator in the 'box had detected and answered correctly. "OK put back" was ordered, again the points shifted across followed by the characteristic shriek that these hydraulic pumps seemed to let out. "Normal" came the cry down the 'phone. "Are we done?" asked Trevor in the 'box. "There's only one problem" said Bob Finch, the lineman, "those points are reverse!" He had spotted, as I had failed to do, that the points were in fact being detected in the opposite position to their actual status – a very hideous 'wrong-side' failure indeed. Fortunately he was a talented man and quickly remedied the situation. The microswitch unit had been connected incorrectly in the factory where it was set up, and all that was needed was a pair of wires to be swapped over for everything to function as it should. The importance of local knowledge (especially as the lie of those points is unusual) and

The operating floor at Ledbury contains a rather bleak frame with a lot of 'white' on display. The Tokenless Block instrument, which utilises a WR single block indicator case, is in the middle of the shelf, showing TRAIN IN SECTION. The white indicator, below the instrument, relays the tip from the guard that the train has arrived 'complete with tail-lamp'. There is a wooden padlocked box on the shelf which contains the handle to manually pump the motor points over. In the event of a failure the signalman may need to go out and do this to keep trains moving. During an extended failure a points operator may be employed to move the points to the signalman's instructions.

thorough testing (as was carried out that day) cannot be underestimated.

The frame in Ledbury signalbox is a GW double Twist, which must be rather old, although it has been converted to 3 bar VT locking. There are 42 levers, the vast majority of which are now white, and unlike anywhere else on the district, there is a lever No. 0. The Up distant has been added to the frame at the correct position – the extreme left of the frame. Rather than shuffle all the other levers along one it is simpler to add a lever and when the GW did this at the left end of the frame it was numbered 0. After zero letters A and B were apparently used by some companies, but this is the only example of a number 'less than one' on the WR today. Nowadays switches are used for additional signals and on the WR seem to get numbered in the 1xx or 2xx series, as we have seen with the CCTV crossings on the Cotswolds.

Ledbury is a slow and steady job, which seems to suit the regulars there who never seem to leave. It's not the scene of much drama, although it has been known for passengers to protest when their train is cancelled there, to return to Worcester in its booked path, leaving the people

wanting Hereford, and the people waiting at Hereford, stranded. Once, the crowd aboard such a train quite rightly refused to alight. Eventually they were taken forward to their destination and I'm told the practice of turning trains in service at Ledbury is now avoided wherever possible (power to the people!) The gate surrounding the 'box steps protects the signalmen from rioting passengers – a luxury we never had on the Cotswolds, although we always seemed able to placate the fury with definitive information. The signalman does have one small duty here which can help on the unmanned platforms. There is a tannoy system rigged up to the 'box on which announcements about delays and suchlike can be made to those waiting below. One relief man told me "Oh I never use that thing if I can help it". I replied that we'd be glad of one at Moreton-in-Marsh where the people queue at the 'box door to be informed, *one at a time!* It was at Ledbury (on the day of the microswitch fiasco) that I achieved a childish, secret whim of mine and was allowed to make the station announcement for the London train, naming all the stations en route with which I had become so familiar.

13

The Neighbours

For a complete record of the patch, I think it appropriate to include a brief description of the neighbouring signalboxes, all of which are very different to anything you'd find at Worcester.

At the western extremity is Hereford, working to Ledbury as detailed in the previous chapter, since the abolition of Shelwick Jct 'box. The remaining 'box at Hereford (Ayleston Hill) is on the south end of Hereford Station. It dates from 1884 and is of joint GW/LNW design which I think, is rather attractive. The whole area was resignalled in the early '70s but undertaken in a very different manner to the work done at Worcester. All the mainline signals are colour light, although the points and discs close to the 'box are mechanically worked. Any remote connections to sidings etc. are controlled from Ground Frames released from the main signalbox. Unlike other regions, the WR still cared for aesthetics in mechanical 'boxes right through rationalisation. So the diagram, the block instruments, indicators and the lever plates are all to the same Reading standard as those we have seen at Worcester. The 1938 GW frame, now of 60 levers, is well cared for and it is only the short handles which indicate that this is quite a modern installation. Eleven years later things were done very differently, so the incongruous panel that works Shelwick Jct to the north, and the tokenless block to Ledbury is a 'one control switch' panel in the ubiquitous vile green shade, which sits at the end of the block shelf. Hereford works AB to Tram Inn signalbox (towards Newport) and AB from Shelwick Jct to Moreton-on-Lugg on the Up line, and TCB throughout on the Down Main line. I have no photo to include of Hereford's interior, because in 10 years of visiting signalboxes (nearly 200 at the last count) this is the only place in Great Britain where the duty signaller totally refused to allow me in the 'box. And it was one of the rare visits that had been pre-arranged with officialdom!

The Midland region meets the Worcester patch at Cutnall Green, between Droitwich Spa and Hartlebury. Hartlebury Station signalbox holds the distinction of being the oldest signalbox in Worcestershire, being a McKenzie and Holland type 2 design from 1876. The MR did not sympathetically modernise their portion of the OWW. In 1982 the lever frame and gatewheel were removed and replaced by a 'chip shop' individual function switch panel – so called because from the rear it resembles a chip shop fryer display unit. A similar job was undertaken at Churchill & Blakedown. The block instruments and barrier controls are integrated into the panel, along with switches for the two home signals, one crossover and associated shunt signal, and the G.F. release at Elmley Lovett siding (now disused) – so the signalman at Hartlebury need never move from his chair.

To the north and south the Worcester patch 'fringes' to Gloucester PSB at Norton Jct and Stoke Works Jct. The 1968 panel signalbox at Gloucester demonstrates the other extreme in WR resignalling. At its opening it would have been an impressive scheme indeed and ultra modern. The panel itself is of the 'N-X' (entrance-exit) type with 'turn and press' switches, as used by the WR in the '60s/70s panels with interchangeable segments, or 'dominos'. One signalman, at the 'A' position, controls trains from Blackwell, at the top of the Lickey incline through Cheltenham Spa station. Another, the 'B' man, controls the triangle surrounding Gloucester and the station itself. And the third controls the main route south to Berkley Road Jct, the single line through the Stroud Valley, and the south Wales line to Awre crossing (not far from Lydney). As well as the two mechanical 'boxes on the Worcester patch, Gloucester works TCB to Saltley (Birmingham), Newport, Bristol and Swindon A panel signalboxes. All these PSBs have train describer screens, so the headcode of a train passes along

Inside Gloucester PSB, Adam Sutton, with whom I worked on the Cotswold line, keeps watch over his area of control. It can be appreciated from this view that to the mechanically minded brain, the panel is a mass of meaningless bright lights and buttons!

Hartlebury Station Signalbox where the Stourbridge District begins. With the exception of Kidderminster Junction, all the boxes on this route have lost their levers.

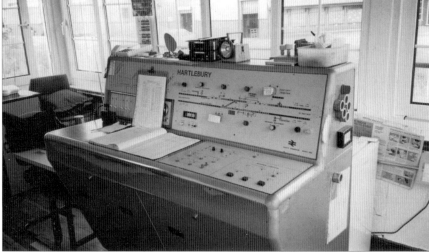

The mini panel at Hartlebury. On the right hand end of the panel are magnetic reminder rings used in similar fashion to lever collars.

from one section to another automatically and onto the next 'box. The controller at Swindon can also see exactly what is where. It is not all 'hi-tech' equipment though. Crossing keepers are retained, in traditional signalboxes (albeit with electric equipment) at Alstone (Cheltenham), Oddingley, Ley and St.Marys (Brimscombe). The latter three all have manually swung gates.

The building itself, along with the other WR PSBs of this era represent the height of architectural ugliness as far as I'm concerned – no doubt functionality was intended. At least this one has large windows, as it must oversee the busy crossing at Horton Road. There is a control pedestal (like those at Newland or Henwick) adjacent to the window, so unusually for a PSB, the signalman can directly see the trains and the people in the immediate vicinity.

In 1973, the same year that Worcester had its mechanical frames and semaphores reconditioned, (and Hereford had colour lights attached to its levers) Oxford had its busy signalboxes destroyed. A small one-man panel now controls the area from Heyford to Radley. Although the area of control is geographically small, it is an area of intensive operations, with a busy station and depot at Oxford and a freight yard at Hinksey. A chap who had trained with me at Evesham 'box, went on to work at Oxford and I joined him there one evening to see what

went on. I was amazed at the hustle and bustle of the place, well into the night, but thought the whole scene was lacking in any ambience. The only nice thing about Oxford PSB is that the relay room is immediately in rear of the panel, so you can hear all the relays respond with clicks and clunks when a route is called. The panel is of the 'N-X' type with push buttons, that may be pulled to cancel a route. My S&T lineman always insisted the panel had come from the short lived WR PSB at Birmingham Snow Hill, although the signal box directory lists it as being second hand from Twyford. Either way, it is not new, and was adapted for Oxford's layout. To the north the 'box fringes to Banbury South, which has a panel to work Aynho Jct, since that 'box's abolition. To the south it fringes to Swindon B Integrated Electronic Control Centre – WR's newest baby in 1993, which was supposed to take over the region, but only managed to pinch the Didcot area from Reading PSB in the end! Oxford also controls the line to Bicester Town by Tokenless Block, which continues onto the freight only line to Claydon L&NE Jct, and finally the Morris Cowley branch which is controlled by traditional tokens with driver worked instruments (NSKT-No Signalman Key Token). The building itself is a ground floor room at the Ascott end of the down platform – if you didn't know where to look you would never guess there was a signalbox there.

EPILOGUE

After my one and only day at Newland East, I returned to the city for my regular week of late turns. However on arriving at Shrub Hill that Monday afternoon, I was greeted by a different inspector who wished to ask me some questions regarding the incidents at Shrub Hill Jct. How had the same signal been passed at danger, twice, on my shift? Obviously he was not satisfied with my response because I was sent to Bristol to be interrogated by a higher authority. I was not concerned, because I knew I had done no different to anyone else and had certainly not been the cause of any mishap. I went, not to the oak panelled Brunellian rooms befitting the Bristol Divisional Operating Superintendent, but to a glass cube within an office complex belonging to a mobile telecommunications company. There, it was decided that I would be sent away from the Worcester patch to work out of the way, for reasons which remain unexplained. I was escorted back to the Station 'box to collect my belongings. Dave Pagett, who had welcomed me to Evesham signalbox as a work experience pupil all those years before, was on duty at the time. We were both unusually quiet – I suppose neither knew what to say under the circumstances. Mr. Gardner was there and asked if I intended to remove the brass plates from the block shelf, which I had actually bought. However it didn't seem right to strip the signalbox of its adornments on account of my untimely departure. He bid me farewell, adding how sorry he was to see me go, and shook me by the hand.

Driving along the M5 everyday, for a 12 hour shift at a level crossing in deepest rural Gloucestershire was not to be endured for long. The railway, to whom I had given all my working life thus far, did not want me anymore and so with heavy heart it was time to hang up my lever cloth for the last time. A new life in the West Highlands of Scotland beckoned, so I left the railway one hot, sunny day in the summer of 2004. My last shift was at St. Mary's crossing, near Stroud – another remnant of the GWR still in existence, with its resident crossing keeper in the adjacent cottage. At least I never suffered the indignity of working a power signalling installation! I had assumed I'd do the job until the signalboxes pegged out (or I did – whichever came first). In reality I did just short of 6 years service with the company since leaving school, of which I was, and still am, very proud.

I only had two ambitions really as a youngster. I wanted to drive a train along the GW mainline, and I wanted to work as a signalman in one of the last steam-age signalboxes left on the network. At Worcester I achieved both of these things, and all before my coming of age. Despite the looming axe of progress and the tyranny of modern management I found there towards the end, I will always think fondly of the place. It was virtually home for a couple of years, and all it takes is a sniff of Lea & Perrin's Worcester Sauce, or the bright ting of the GW bell at my front door and I am transported back to those busy days and nights at Worcester Shrub Hill, keeping the trains and the blissfully ignorant British public safely on the move.

Acknowledgements

In publishing this book about the Worcester Signalboxes I would like to salute all those railway people with whom I worked, many of whom still perform the duties detailed within these pages. Without the friendly signalmen, train drivers and guards, station staff, S&T and permanent way engineers I encountered over the last 10 years there wouldn't be anything worth writing about – they are the characters who bring these splendid old places to life. So, thanks to you all.

Many thanks are due to all those who have assisted me with this project, by allowing access to take photographs, confirming dates and so on. I am especially indebted to the following who have contributed greatly to the finished article: The Worcester Signalmen's Inspectorate, Paul Hale, Richard Morgan and Adrian Putley for providing photographs, Ray Casson (of the Signalling Record Society) and Kevin Simpson for his superb diagrams, Kathy Whitaker-Shepherd and Philip Elwell for unfailing help with the text.

Sources consulted:

Signalling Atlas and Directory by Peter Kay and Derek Coe
Quail Track Diagrams by TRACKmaps publications
Railway Rulebook published by the RSSB
Accident investigations (for Worcester Tunnel Jct) available on the internet
Article by B.Bennett (SRS Signalling Record) on WR prefabricated signalboxes
Track Layout Diagrams by R.A.Cooke. Section 28 & 33
GWR Signalbox Nameplates by Michael.V.E.Dunn
SRS Signalbox directory, kindly provided by R.Casson

Network Rail
Worcester Depot

Previous page - *No. 76 / 77, Up Platform line to (down) Up Main Starting or Down Branch. The mechanical route indicator displays B'HAM or H'FRD depending upon the route selected. Behind the signal is the S & T maintenance depot where I served my apprenticeship.*

This page top left - *'Bells and Brasso' at Norton Junction.*

This page bottom - *The 84 lever frame at Worcester Shrub Hill Station signal box, is one of the most impressive survivors from the steam era.*

Top left - *Newland East is the only 'box for miles around without an illuminated diagram, which meant pinching it was a simple case of lifting it off the ceiling hooks. Irritatingly someone did just that (at least no official reason for its removal was ever discovered) and replaced it with a nasty computer generated design seen here. Even worse than that – the new diagram is incorrect!*

Top right - *Worcester Tunnel Junction signals: Loco Shed to Down Main, (No. 35) and the Down Main home (No. 17). It was confusion between these two signals that caused a train to hit the buffer stops, see page 67.*

Bottom - *The 'new' lever No. 68 in Droitwich Spa Signal Box, now controlling Fernhill Heath Intermediate Block signals, see text page 74. The lever has a short handle reminding the signalman not to exert undue force. As the actual signals are colour light the lever is, in effect, a large switch, as is its neighbour, which controls motorised points.*

Above - Worcester Shrub Hill Junction. This whole area was formerly covered in a maze of sidings and various railway buildings. Most have gone, fortunately the semaphore signals remain.

Right - Modern trains at Evesham await the single line token. As a boy, I recall walking with Dad over the same bridge and witnessing similar scenes.